Defiant Earth

Defiant Earth
The Fate of Humans in the Anthropocene

Clive Hamilton

polity

Copyright © Clive Hamilton 2017

The right of Clive Hamilton to be identified as Author of this Work has been asserted in accordance with the UK Copyright, Designs and Patents Act 1988.

First published in 2017 by Polity Press

Polity Press
65 Bridge Street
Cambridge CB2 1UR, UK

Polity Press
350 Main Street
Malden, MA 02148, USA

ISBN-13: 978-1-5095-1974-3
ISBN-13: 978-1-5095-1975-0(pb)

A catalogue record for this book is available from the British Library.

Typeset in 11 on 14.5pt Adobe Garamond Pro by
Servis Filmsetting Limited, Stockport, Cheshire
Printed and bound in the UK by CPI Group (UK) Ltd, Croydon

The publisher has used its best endeavours to ensure that the URLs for external websites referred to in this book are correct and active at the time of going to press. However, the publisher has no responsibility for the websites and can make no guarantee that a site will remain live or that the content is or will remain appropriate.

Every effort has been made to trace all copyright holders, but if any have been inadvertently overlooked the publisher will be pleased to include any necessary credits in any subsequent reprint or edition.

For further information on Polity, visit our website:
politybooks.com

Contents

CONTENTS

Preface:
On Waking Up

This is not a book of warning; it is a book groping toward an understanding of what it means after 200,000 years of modern humans on a 4.5 billion-year-old Earth to have arrived at this point in history, the Anthropocene. I say "groping toward" because the change has come upon us with disorienting speed. It is the kind of shift that typically takes two or three or four generations to sink in. Our best scientists tell us insistently that a calamity is unfolding, that the life-support systems of the Earth are being damaged in ways that threaten our survival. Yet in the face of these facts we carry on as usual. Most citizens ignore or downplay the warnings; many of our intellectuals indulge in wishful thinking; and some influential voices declare that nothing at all is happening, that the scientists are deceiving us. Yet the evidence tells us that so powerful have humans become that we have entered a new and dangerous geological epoch, defined by the fact that the "human imprint on the global environment has now become so large and active that it rivals some of the great forces of Nature in its impact on the functioning of the Earth system."[1]

This bizarre situation, in which we have become potent

enough to change the course of the Earth yet seem unable to regulate ourselves, contradicts every modern belief about the kind of
creature the human being is. So for some it is absurd to suggest
that humankind could break out of the boundaries of history
and inscribe itself as a geological force in deep time. Humans are
too puny to change the climate, they insist, so it is outlandish
to suggest we could change the Geological Time Scale. Others
assign the Earth and its evolution to the divine realm so that it is
not merely impertinence to suggest that humans can overrule the
Almighty but blasphemy. Many intellectuals in the social sciences
and humanities do not concede that Earth scientists have anything to say that could impinge on their understanding of the
world, because the "world" consists only of humans engaging with
humans, with nature no more than a passive backdrop to draw on
as we please. The "humans-only" orientation of the social sciences
and humanities is reinforced in "mediatized" societies where total
absorption in representations of reality derived from various forms
of media encourages us to view the ecological crisis as a spectacle
that takes place outside the bubble of our existence.

It is true that grasping the scale of what is happening requires
not only breaking the bubble but also making the cognitive leap to
Earth System thinking. It is one thing to accept that human influence has spread across the landscape, the oceans, and the atmosphere, but quite another to make the jump to understanding that
human activities are disrupting the functioning of the Earth as
a complex, dynamic, ever-evolving totality comprised of myriad
interlocking processes. But consider this astounding fact.

With knowledge of the cycles that govern Earth's rotation,
including its tilt and wobble, paleo-climatologists are able to

predict with reasonable certainty that the next ice age is due in 50,000 years' time.[2] Yet because carbon dioxide persists in the atmosphere for millennia, global warming from human activity in the twentieth and twenty-first centuries is expected to *suppress* that ice age and quite possibly the following one, expected (other things being equal) in 130,000 years. If human activity occurring over a century or two can irreversibly transform the global climate for tens of thousands of years, we are prompted to rethink history and social analysis as a purely intra-human affair.

How should we understand the disquieting fact that a mass of scientific evidence about the Anthropocene, an unfolding event of colossal proportions, has been insufficient to induce a reasoned and fitting response? For many, the accumulation of facts about ecological disruption seems to have a narcotizing effect, all too apparent in popular attitudes to the crisis of the Earth System, and especially among opinion-makers and political leaders. A few have opened themselves to the full meaning of the Anthropocene, crossing a threshold by way of a gradual but ever-more disturbing process of evidence-assimilation or, in some cases, after a realization that breaks over them suddenly and with great force in response to an event or piece of information in itself quite small.

In German, *Erlebnis* can simply mean an event or occurrence in the course of life, the type of personal experience that was the hallmark of nineteenth-century Romanticism's appeal to feeling. But it can also refer to an intense disruptive episode, one that makes an indelible impression, changing a life course, the kind of experience not so much integrated into a life but which relegates the old life to the past and inaugurates a new sensibility, "something unforgettable and irreplaceable, something whose meaning cannot be exhausted by conceptual determination."³ Such a realization is not only a powerful emotional event but also one saturated with meaning. The subject often has the inexplicable feeling that the event has some purpose that asks to be understood. It is as if some force has intervened, creating a rupture that has meaning beyond the personal, a universal truth. And so beyond the science as such, the few alert to the plight of the Earth sense that something unfathomably great is taking place, "suffused with what is coming,"⁴ conscious that we face a struggle between ruin and the possibility of some kind of salvation.

So today the greatest tragedy is the absence of a sense of the tragedy. The indifference of most to the Earth System's disturbance may be attributed to a failure of reason or psychological weaknesses; but these seem inadequate to explain why we find ourselves on the edge of the abyss. How can we understand the miserable failure of contemporary thinking to come to grips with what now confronts us? A few years after the second atomic bomb was dropped, Kazuo Ishiguro wrote a novel about the people of Nagasaki, a novel in which the bomb is never mentioned yet whose shadow falls over everyone. The Anthropocene's shadow too falls over all of us. Yet the bookshops are regularly replenished with tomes about world futures from our leading intellectuals of left and right in which the ecological crisis is barely mentioned. They write about the rise of China, clashing civilizations, and machines that take over the world, composed and put forward as if climate scientists do not exist. They prognosticate about a future from which the dominant facts have been expunged, futurologists trapped in an obsolete past. It is the great silence. At a dinner party one of Europe's most eminent psychoanalysts held forth ardently on every topic but fell mute when climate change was raised. He had nothing to say. For most of the intelligentsia, it is as if the projections of Earth scientists are so preposterous they can safely be ignored. Perhaps the intellectual surrender is so complete because the forces we hoped would make the world a more civilized place – personal freedoms, democracy, material advance, technological power – are in truth paving the way to its destruction. The powers we most trusted have betrayed us; that which we believed would save us now threatens to devour us. For some, the tension is resolved by rejecting the evidence, which is to say, by discarding the Enlightenment. For others, the response is to denigrate calls to heed the danger as a loss of faith in humanity, as if anguish for the Earth were a romantic illusion or superstitious regression. Yet the Earth scientists continue to haunt us, following us around like wailing apparitions while we hurry on with our lives, turning round occasionally with irritation to hold up the crucifix of Progress.

Acknowledgments

Over three or four years this short book has been through several drafts, some radically different from their predecessors. I keep shifting my views, partly because when pushing at the boundaries of one's understanding breakthroughs periodically occur, but more so because colleagues have pointed out contradictions, mistakes, and foolish detours. I feel privileged to be the beneficiary of many of my colleagues' willingness to share their extraordinary knowledge, but if my intellectual debts are mountainous, then, unlike monetary ones, they are not onerous because they have been accumulated through so much generosity.

Many of the ideas in this book have emerged in the course of an engagement over the last few years with Bruno Latour, who did me the honour of reading two entire drafts. They were bruising encounters, but deeply provoking and sympathetic to the project and a quite different book emerged as a result.

Bron Szerszynski read an early draft and was kind enough to point me in some fruitful directions. Lisa Sideris provided a truly thought-provoking commentary that helped me resolve some weaknesses and contradictions in the argument. Adrian Wilding read certain key sections and was especially helpful with the philosophical references in the text. My friend Kjell Anderson read an early draft and provided a boost. Stephen Muecke posed some awkward questions to which I have tried to respond. Two anonymous readers provided both encouragement and challenges.

Conversations and email exchanges with an ever-generous Will Steffen have greatly extended and deepened my grasp of Earth System science. Jan Zalasiewicz has set me straight on various aspects of the science. My understanding of the development of this new science has been heavily influenced by my association with Jacques Grinevald, a wise collaborator who helped me see many things more clearly.

Dipesh Chakrabarty generously took time out from his pressured academic life to read a draft and pose challenging questions that forced me to make some big changes. His intellectual influence can readily be seen in the text. Thought-provoking exchanges with Alf Hornborg, Christophe Bonneuil, and Ingolfur Blühdorn helped shape my ideas, strengthen the arguments, and provide impetus to develop the ideas further.

My colleagues Stephen Pickard, Scott Cowdell, and Wayne Hudson very kindly gave their time and wisdom when they read a draft and told me of its weaknesses and strengths. My daily association with them at George Browning House is a blessing, for they create a rich and open-minded intellectual environment. Finally, I must thank Charles Sturt University for providing me with the freedom and support to pursue a speculative project like this one.

ACKNOWLEDGMENTS

While the published text has been improved beyond measure as a result of the commentaries and advice from those I have mentioned, none is responsible for any of the remaining views.

1 The Anthropocene Rupture

A rupture in Earth history

First, the science. The Geological Time Scale divides the Earth's history into ages, epochs, periods, eras, and eons in ascending order of significance. The International Commission on Stratigraphy is considering officially adding a new epoch, the Anthropocene, to the scale. Stratigraphers – geologists who specialize in the study of rock layering – are perhaps the most tradition-bound members of a somewhat conservative profession; yet their decision has the most radical implications.

The principal reason for Earth scientists' belief that the planet has shifted out of the previous epoch, the Holocene, lies in the rapid increase in the concentration of carbon dioxide in the atmosphere and its cascading effects throughout the Earth System. The system-changing forces of ocean acidification, species loss, and disruption of the nitrogen cycle add to the case. Human disturbance of the climate system is now detectable from the beginning of large-scale coal burning at the onset of the Industrial Revolution. The rise in atmospheric concentrations of carbon dioxide was gradual for the next 150 years, but became steep after World War II. Now a range of indicators shows sharp and unambiguous human disturbance to the Earth System from the end of World War II.[1] The post-war period stands out, writes Earth scientist Will Steffen, "as one of the most remarkable in all of human history for its rapidity and pervasiveness of change."[2] Other Earth System scientists express it a little differently: "The last 60 years have without doubt seen the most profound transformation of the human relationship with the natural world in the history of humankind."[3]

Long-term trends in global economic growth, resource use, and waste volumes show a sharp upturn after World War II, a period dubbed the "Great Acceleration" and that continues today. For this reason, expert opinion now dates the beginning of the new epoch from around 1945 rather than the end of the eighteenth century as first proposed.[4] From a strictly stratigraphic point of view (the one most germane to the official decision on the new epoch), a million years hence the sharpest marker in the rock record will be the sudden deposition of radionuclides across the Earth's surface as a result of nuclear explosions in 1945, known as the "bomb spike." Although the nuclear age has not itself changed the functioning of the Earth System, the layer of radionuclides laid down in 1945 does mark the dawn of the era of US global hegemony and the astounding period of material expansion of the post-war decades, that is, of capitalism's sublime success. We now understand what that success meant for the Earth System. It is measured most simply and strikingly by the Keeling Curve, showing the secular increase in carbon dioxide concentrations in the atmosphere. Earth scientist James Syvitski puts it succinctly:

2

"By any unbiased and quantitative measure humans have affected the surface of the Earth at a magnitude that ice ages have had on our planet, but over a much shorter period of time."[5] The course of the Earth System has been changed irrevocably.

To understand why these changes are effectively permanent consider global warming alone. Humans have redistributed the Earth System's stock of carbon, a vital element that profoundly affects the climate. Large reserves of carbon that had over millions of years been immobilized as fossils deep beneath the Earth's surface have been dug up, burned, and released in the system, where they will remain mobile in the atmosphere, oceans, and biosphere. It will probably be hundreds of thousands of years before most of this carbon can be rendered immobile again. In the meantime, the pulse of carbon dioxide emitted into the atmosphere over a century or two is bringing changes that have everlasting consequences. Because they naturally draw carbon dioxide out of the atmosphere, the oceans are already a third more acidic than they were before humans began burning fossil fuels on a large scale. Over a time-scale of many thousands of years, rising acidity disturbs the natural process of deposition of calcium carbonate on the deep seafloor.[6] The destabilization of ice masses, such as glaciers and the Greenland ice-sheet, is not something that can be reversed except over tens of thousands of years. The possibility of an ice-free Earth over the next few centuries, bringing much higher sea levels, cannot be ruled out. Such a reconfiguration of the Earth System can be undone only over many millennia, if at all. In the words of 22 earth scientists writing in *Nature*, "the next few decades offer a brief window of opportunity to minimize [but not prevent] large-scale and potentially catastrophic climate change that will extend longer than the entire history of human civilization thus far."[7]

A long time after humans disappear, or shrink to a position where we are no longer interfering in the Earth System, the great processes that drive planetary change – orbital forcing, plate tectonics, volcanism, natural evolution, and so on – will overwhelm human influences. But the planet will not settle into a state that looks anything like the Holocene – the 10,000-year epoch of mild and constant climate that permitted civilization to flourish. It has been diverted onto a different trajectory. Experts are already suggesting that the changes caused by humans in recent decades are so profound and long-lasting that we have entered not a new epoch but a new *era* – the Anthropozoic era – on a par with the break in Earth history brought by the arrival of multicellular life.[8]

So 1945 marks the turning point in the sweep of Earth's history at which the geological evolution of the planet diverged from one driven by blind forces of nature to one influenced by a conscious, willing being, a new human-geological power. We are accustomed to the idea of humans as the agents that make history, and use the term "pre-history" for the period from the emergence of early humans to the invention of writing. Now we must concede what seemed impossible to contemplate – humans as agents changing the course of the *deep* history of the Earth, or rather of the Earth's deep future, an event giving rise to what might be called "post-history."

Although we are preoccupied with what the Anthropocene may mean for the future of humans, the present decades mark a transition in which Earth's biogeological history itself enters a new phase, because the Earth's history has become entangled with human history so that *"the fate of one determines the fate of the other."*[9] In a few short decades we have seen the entire history of the Earth – from its formation through to its eventual vaporization when the Sun finally explodes – split irrevocably into two halves – the first 4.5 billion years in which Earth history was determined by blind natural forces alone, and the remaining 5 billion years in which it will be influenced by a conscious power long after that power is spent. If humans disappear, then the great forces that drive the Earth System will continue and eventually erase the more obvious impacts of humans on the landscape. Even so, signs of the influence of humankind – its rise, fall, and enduring legacy – will be evident, not least in a disturbance in the rock record, a freakish band of a few hundred thousand years somewhere in the middle of the 10 billion-year record of the Earth.

Volition in nature

In all previous instances, transitions from one division to the next in the Geological Time Scale came about because of the gradual evolution of natural forces or, at times, a single massive event. These forces are unconscious and unintentional so that the feedback effects from one element to another are not filtered but exert their influence directly (albeit in complex ways). However, if the human imprint on the Earth System is so far-reaching that *Homo sapiens* now competes with the forces of nature in its impact on the way the planet as a whole functions, the human imprint is the effect of a force fundamentally unlike physical ones such as weathering, volcanism, asteroid strike, subduction, and solar fluxes. This new "force of nature" contains something radically different – the element of volition.

Global anthropogenic impacts, such as increases in carbon dioxide in the atmosphere and disturbance to the nitrogen cycle, do not just happen but are the consequences, intended or otherwise, of *decisions* taken by human minds. In nature, as we have always understood it, the forces of nature are unconscious and involuntary; no decisions are made, so to comprehend humanity as a geological force we need to consider its distinctive quality, its volitional element. Humankind is perhaps better described not as a geological force but as a *geological power*, because we have to consider its ability to make decisions as well as its ability to transform matter. Unlike forces of nature, it is a power that can be withheld as well as exercised.

So for the first time in the Earth's 4.5 billion-year history we have a non-physical force (which brings about physical effects) mixed in with physical forces, although it is not so much *added* to the pre-existing natural forces but in some sense *infuses* them and modifies their operation. And this new force can be integrated only imperfectly into the system of geodynamics used to explain the geological evolution of the planet. The uncertainty about how this new force will behave is the primary reason for the wide variation in projections of global warming over the twenty-first century. And it now seems certain that as long as humans are on the planet all future epochs, eras, periods, and so on will be hybrids of physical forces and this new power. No wonder there has been deep uneasiness in some sections of the geology profession about adding this weird division to official geochronology.

The inference that the Anthropocene is a profoundly new

kind of division in the Geological Time Scale, and that 1945 marks an ontological shift in the deep history of the planet, can be reached another way. In deciding to add the Anthropocene to its geochronology the International Commission on Stratigraphy needs to agree, on the basis of stratigraphic indicators, that it is best classified as a geological *epoch*, as proposed. Some leading scientists are suggesting that deeming it an epoch – longer than an age but shorter than a period – is a conservative but appropriate decision. But they note that if society does not respond soon to the signs of climate disruption, then it may be necessary to upgrade the Anthropocene from an epoch to a period, or even to a new era, the Anthropozoic era, to succeed the current era, the Cenozoic, which began 66 million years ago.[10]

In other words, we are entering a geological episode whose designation depends not only on gathering and evaluating the available data, but also on human impacts on the Earth System that *have not yet occurred*. The verdict on the Anthropocene reached by the International Commission on Stratigraphy could be invalidated not by the *discovery* of new evidence that already exists, but by the *generation* of new evidence that may appear in the next few decades. That is impossible for every previous decision concerning the Geological Time Scale. The new geological epoch is radically distinct from all previous ones, so that 1945 may be thought of as the boundary that marks a break in Earth history of the greatest profundity; it divides the life span of Earth into two halves ontologically. In other words, the being-nature of the object itself has changed.

The historian Dipesh Chakrabarty has made the striking observation, pregnant with implications, that the arrival of the

Anthropocene means that human history and geological history have converged, calling into question the modern conception of history as, in Jacob Burckhardt's words, "the break with nature caused by the awakening of consciousness."[11] The initial divergence of the two histories can be traced to the emergence of the science of geology in the eighteenth century. Acceptance of its implications was slow. In the 1854 edition of *Encyclopaedia Britannica* we find "A Chronological Table from the Creation of the World to the Year 1854." It begins: "B.C. 4004 Creation of the World, according to the Hebrew text of the Scriptures." After centuries in which the European story of humans was part of the story of the Earth in the cosmology of Genesis, or similar myths of cosmogenesis in other cultures, it was geology's discovery that the Earth is much older than humans, indeed much older than life, that gave the Earth its own history. It was only after nature acquired its own history that humans could acquire a history in the modern sense. An understanding of an independent human history became the foundation of all modern social sciences, so the convergence – or better, the collision – of human and Earth histories in the Anthropocene kindles the suspicion that all social sciences and their philosophical foundations have been built on an understanding of the historical process that is no longer defensible.

The convergence means that, contrary to our attempts to make ourselves free of the natural world, our future is tied to the fate of the Earth. Our disturbance of the Earth System has rendered it more unstable and unpredictable. Whereas industrialism's essential aim has been to bring the natural world under human supervision, in practice the effect has been to leave it *less* controllable. If, as climatologist Kevin Trenberth has written, "all weather events are affected by [human-induced] climate change because the environment in which they occur is warmer and moister than it used to be,"[12] every extreme event now has a human fingerprint. Flood, famine, fire, and pestilence can no longer be purely natural, so the theological distinction (also commonplace among the secular) between moral evil and natural evil collapses. What, we might now ask, does it mean to write insurance policies exempting the insurer from liability for "acts of God"? Humankind is now confronted with a momentous decision: to attempt to exert *more* control so as to subdue the Earth with greater technological power – the express purpose of some forms of geoengineering – or to draw back and practice meekness, with all of the social consequences that would follow.

Earth System science

The idea of the Anthropocene was conceived by Earth System scientists to capture the very recent rupture in Earth history arising from the impact of human activity on the Earth System as a whole.

I ask the reader to stop and read the above sentence again, taking special note of the phrases "very recent rupture" and "the Earth System as a whole." Understanding the Anthropocene, and what humanity now confronts, is entirely dependent on a firm grasp of these concepts. As we will see, "the Anthropocene" has quickly become so encrusted with misreadings, misconceptions, and ideological co-optations that most who come to it for the first time are liable to be seriously misled. It is of the utmost importance to understand that the "Anthropocene" is not a term coined to describe the continued spread of human impacts on the landscape or further modification to ecosystems; it is instead a term describing a *rupture* in the functioning of the Earth System as a whole, so much so that the Earth has now entered a new geological epoch.

Whatever conclusions one might draw as to the ultimate causes and the solutions to the Anthropocene, an understanding of the basic science of it must come first. Such an understanding requires not much more than a careful reading of the half-dozen seminal papers in scientific journals, and yet most who lurch into print on the subject have not taken the time. (Ian Angus has now provided a superb overview of the science in the first part of his book *Facing the Anthropocene*.[13])

First named by atmospheric chemist Paul Crutzen in the year 2000, the Anthropocene is the name for a proposed new epoch to be added to the official Geological Time Scale that segments the entire history of the Earth.[14] As we saw, the scale is divided into ages, epochs, periods, eras, and eons, like Russian dolls, with "ages" as the smallest. The Anthropocene epoch succeeds the Holocene, the one that for the last 10,000 years has given the Earth a remarkably clement and stable climate.

It became possible to conceive the idea of a human-induced rupture in the functioning of the Earth System only after the development of the new scientific paradigm of Earth System science, the roots of which lie in new strands of scientific thinking dating from the 1970s and 1980s that coalesced in the 1990s. Those strands included: the application of systems modeling to Earth's resources by Meadows and others in the 1970s; James Lovelock's Gaia hypothesis, first advanced in 1979; early biophysical modeling of the Earth's biosphere in the 1980s; the startling results of

Antarctic ice-core drilling in the same decade; the formation of the International Geosphere-Biosphere Programme in 1983–6; and the creation of the Intergovernmental Panel on Climate Change in 1988.[15] We might also mention the impact of the images of the Earth taken from space by the Apollo space missions in the late 1960s, although they are subject to readings other than the usual romantic one.

The concept of the Anthropocene applies to the new object of the *Earth System,* an object that only came into view in the 1980s and 1990s with the emergence of Earth System science. This claim may seem implausible. Haven't scientists, and before them natural philosophers, conceived of the Earth as a functioning system for much longer, perhaps as early as the eighteenth century? No. A globe with a crust and some biota on it does not a system make. It's worth noting that the notion of a *global* climate (one of the components of the Earth System) became widely accepted by scientists only after World War II. Except for a few speculative commentaries, "climate" had previously been considered a local and regional phenomenon. In the nineteenth century "the climate" was understood as the long-term average of the weather in a region or country. A popular handbook still being published in 1961 argued that "the notion of a global climate made little sense" because the weather is too changeable between the poles and the tropics.[16] Until the 1970s climatology was a profession limited in size and mostly found in geography departments, one that confined itself to the compilation of statistics on regional weather.[17]

The new Earth System thinking that emerged fully in the 1990s and 2000s is the integrative meta-science of the whole planet understood as a unified, complex, evolving system beyond the sum of its parts. It is a transdisciplinary and holistic approach assimilating earth sciences and life sciences, as well as the "industrial metabolism" of humankind, all within a systems way of thinking, with special focus on the non-linear dynamics of a system.[18] It represents a markedly novel way of thinking about the Earth that supersedes ecological thinking.[19] The latter, which emerged fully in the 1960s and 1970s, is the biological science of the relationships among organisms and between communities of organisms and their local environments. Ecology studies the local and regional; Earth System science studies the Earth as a total system.

Crucially, the new concept of the Earth System encompasses and transcends previous objects of study such as "the landscape," "ecosystems," and "the environment"; it is the Earth taken as a whole in a constant state of movement driven by interconnected cycles and forces, from the planet's core to the atmosphere and out to the Moon, and powered by the flow of energy from the Sun. It is a single, dynamic, integrated system, and *not* a collection of ecosystems.

As we will see, a great deal of confusion arises from the elision of the new object of the Earth System with these earlier objects of study. Rather than Earth System thinking displacing ecological thinking, it is more correct to say that Earth System science is the name for systematic thinking about the new object of the Earth System, which is not the same object to which ecological thinking is properly applied. The gulf between the two remains even when the local environments of ecological thinking are aggregated up to the "global environment"; the global environment thought this way is not the Earth System. The Anthropocene is emphatically not a new name for a more intense phase of human disturbance of local and regional ecosystems. The concept was envisioned in 2000 to capture the qualitative leap from disturbances of ecosystems to disruption of the Earth System.

Since Thomas Kuhn published his landmark book *The Structure of Scientific Revolutions* in 1962, analysts have been too eager to identify a "paradigm shift" in one area of science or another. Yet it seems to be justified in the case of Earth System science, for if a paradigm is a distinct set of assumptions and patterns of thought, then there can be little doubt that Earth System science meets the criterion.

Scientific misinterpretations

As we will see, most commentary by social scientists on the Anthropocene begins from a mistaken understanding of the science behind the concept. The confusion is perhaps forgivable because much of the analysis from *scientists* begins from the same misconception. Most scientists who go into print on the issue are not Earth System scientists and read the new concept through old disciplinary lenses. If we want to understand the Anthropocene we must listen to the scientists who have learned to think in terms of the Earth System.

The distinctiveness of Earth System science as a paradigm-shifting meta-science has become apparent in debates over various attempts to invent new starting dates for the Anthropocene. These debates have shown up the gulf between Earth System science and traditional geographical, geological, and ecological thinking, which are inadequate when applied to the Earth System as a whole. Grasping the idea of the Earth System – emphasizing the co-evolution of its "spheres," the atmosphere, the hydrosphere (watery parts), the cryosphere (icy parts), the biosphere (life and its surrounds), and the lithosphere (the Earth's crust) – requires a kind of gestalt shift, one big "Aha" moment, or usually several smaller ones. Without it the Earth is understood as the aggregation of ecosystems more or less modified by humans. In the absence of such a gestalt shift it is possible to read the idea of the Anthropocene into older forms of disciplinary thinking in the geological, archaeological, paleo-anthropological, ecological, or human geographical traditions.

And so, soon after the concept was proposed, a number of scientists and social scientists began to put forward interpretations of the Anthropocene that, mostly unwittingly, *deflated* the significance of the new epoch and the threat it poses to humankind and the Earth.

When first proposed by Earth System scientists, it was suggested that the beginning of the Anthropocene should be dated from the late eighteenth century when, due to the large-scale burning of coal, there was a now-detectable increase in greenhouse gases in the atmosphere and so the beginning of modern global warming. In 2003, paleo-climatologist William Ruddiman published a paper arguing that the Holocene–Anthropocene shift occurred not at the end of the eighteenth century with the Industrial Revolution but 5,000–8,000 years ago with the onset of forest clearing and farming, which led to enhanced levels of carbon dioxide and methane in the atmosphere.[20] However, Ruddiman's interpretation of the data turned out to be unpersuasive because human impact on the Earth System (as opposed to the landscape)

5,000 to 8,000 years ago is not discernible in the data, and certainly was not large enough to upset the stability of the Holocene Earth. Reviewing the evidence, the Intergovernmental Panel on Climate Change came to the same conclusion.[21]

Ruddiman's interests were scientific but the dispute has wider implications. One is that if humans have been a planetary force since civilization emerged, then industrialism and the extensive burning of fossil fuels did not represent anything fundamentally new in the human project; nor is it a rupture in Earth history. If humans have been transforming the Earth System for many thousands of years, then it is in our nature to do so. The Anthropocene is therefore a "natural" event rather than the result of certain forms of social organization coupled with techno-industrial hubris. It does not reflect any kind of human failure.

Several scientists have attempted to interpret the Anthropocene as no more than another name for the continued impact of humans on the landscape or ecosystems. Erle Ellis claims that since humans "have been reshaping the terrestrial biosphere" for millennia "the entire past 11,000 years of the Holocene might simply be renamed the Anthropocene."[22] For Earth System scientists the new epoch is presented as a geological epoch *in contrast to* the Holocene. Bizarrely, Ellis defends the view that humans are not a destructive force but have always been "sustained and permanent stewards of the biosphere." (Tell that to the thousands of species humans have extinguished.) None of the leading exponents of Earth System science believes that changes in the terrestrial biosphere alone can bring about a new epoch, and even less so if we are thinking of vegetation and landscape ecology. After considering differing conceptions of the biosphere, two Earth System scientists conclude that "the terrestrial biosphere, in isolation, is not the right place to be looking for a planetary-scale tipping point; one must consider the coupled dynamics of the Earth system as a whole, including evolution."[23]

Elsewhere, Ellis – a landscape ecologist rather than an Earth System scientist – makes a shopping list of human impacts covering domestication of animals, genetic modifications, combustion of fossil carbon, changes to the nitrogen cycle, artificial lighting, soil tillage, nuclear power, earthworks, and transport of materials – all of which "taken together" are "shifting the planet into a new epoch of geologic time; the Anthropocene."[24] Seen this way, the Anthropocene is nothing new and nothing to worry about; indeed, as we will see, Ellis is among a number of political conservatives who *welcome* it.

A view from archaeology on the starting date controversy also begins with a pre-Earth System science understanding. In a paper titled "The Onset of the Anthropocene," published in the journal *Anthropocene*, the abstract begins:

> A number of different starting dates for the Anthropocene epoch have been proposed, reflecting different disciplinary perspectives and criteria regarding when human societies first began to play a significant role in shaping the earth's ecosystems.[25]

One need not read past this sentence to know that the authors have misconstrued the new epoch completely, and that their conclusions about the onset of the new epoch must be mistaken. It's the very last letter, the "s" in ecosystems, that gives it away. The Anthropocene does not begin when humans first play "a significant role in shaping the earth's ecosystems"; it begins when humans first play a significant role in shaping the *Earth*, that is, the Earth that evolves as a totality, as a unified, complex system comprised of the tightly linked atmosphere, hydrosphere, cryosphere, biosphere, and lithosphere. It is not about changes to ecosystems except insofar as ecosystem change is a component of the disruption of the spheres that constitute the Earth System.

The archaeologists argue that "the beginning of the Anthropocene can be usefully defined in terms of when evidence of significant human capacity for ecosystem engineering or niche construction behaviors first appear in the archeological record on a global scale." These behaviors are traced to the domestication of plants and animals beginning 10,000 years ago. In a similar distortion two other archaeologists, peering through their accustomed lens, see the Anthropocene as no more than a part of a "single complex continuum" over 50,000 years due to "human geographic expansion."[26]

If through an archaeological lens some see an Anthropocene in domestication of plants and animals, and through Ellis's landscape ecology lens it is seen in evidence of landscape change, both diminish the significance *and changed nature* of the human impact on the Earth System that the Anthropocene concept captures. Their visions are inclined to lull the reader into the belief that the Anthropocene is no more than an interesting new way of expressing the traditional understanding of the human relationship to the natural environment. Yet the Anthropocene concept would not have been possible without the emergence of Earth System science in the 1980s and 1990s as a way of understanding the novel role of humankind in the Earth System, as distinct from the understanding embedded in traditional environmental science.

It is also possible to misread the nature and significance of the Anthropocene by viewing it through the lens of social geography. In what is known as the "pre-Columbian Anthropocene hypothesis," Simon Lewis and Mark Maslin locate the start of the new epoch in 1610, based on a complex narrative covering the colonization of South America, introduced diseases, depopulation, forest regrowth, transcontinental trade, species exchange, and pollen counts, all of which are said to be associated with a small dip in the atmospheric concentration of carbon dioxide in that year.[27] However, the analysis failed to show numerically that the dip (*sic*) in carbon dioxide changed the functioning of the Earth System or was caused by human activity. A number of Earth System scientists pointed out that in the pre-industrial Holocene there were many comparable dips in the atmospheric carbon dioxide concentration, and that a change of 10 parts per million is well within the range of natural variability in the Holocene, and pales into triviality beside the jump in the concentration from 280 parts per million in 1800 to 400 today.

Finally, soil scientists have entered the debate, arguing that evidence of anthropogenic modification of soils going back 2,000 years defines the start of the Anthropocene.[28] Yet this argument from pedology is also based on a total misconception of the definition of the proposed new epoch, namely: "The Anthropocene is, by definition, the period when human activity acts as a major driving factor, if not the dominant process, in modifying the landscape and the environment." This argument has been taken apart by two other soil scientists. Yet they too reproduce its essential flaw when they interpret the Anthropocene as the initiation of "significant human environmental impact ... on the Earth's surface."[29] To repeat: it's not "the landscape," it's not "the environment," and it's not "the Earth's surface." It's the system as a totality.

That so many scientists, publishing in prestigious journals, can misconstrue the basic definition of the Anthropocene as nothing more than a measure of the "human footprint" on the landscape is a sign of how far Earth System science has to go in changing the way many scientists understand the Earth. A common feature of these misreadings of the Anthropocene through the lenses of ecology, social geography, archaeology, and pedology – that is, by treating the new epoch as a continuation of landscape or ecosystem change going back centuries or millennia – is that they divorce it from modern industrialization and the burning of fossil fuels. In this way they deny that the Anthropocene represents a *rupture* in Earth history, and deprive it of its dangerous quality. It is rendered benign.

Curiously, this scientific misreading of the Anthropocene accords with the views of some analysts in the social sciences and humanities. In their important volume *The Shock of the Anthropocene*, historians Christophe Bonneuil and Jean-Baptiste Fressoz claim that those who speak of the Anthropocene "should not act as astonished ingénues who suddenly discover they are transforming the planet."[30] They write that the new epoch has a "long history" and is in effect another term for "environmental disturbance" so that there were "Anthropocene societies" in the eighteenth century.[31] The argument elides the recent rupture in geochronology with early industrial ecological damage, which effectively denies that anything new has happened. The danger of this approach is that to paint the new situation as no more than a continuation of the past misses the true novelty of the dispensation and invites application of out-of-date social analysis and strategies to a world that has transcended them. The Anthropocene rupture will require original political thinking. To draw an analogy, in the insurrectionary year 1848 Karl Marx would not have argued that one should look to the lessons of peasant revolts for an understanding of the situation or a political response. (Ian Angus presents a Marxist view of the Anthropocene that, whatever one may think of the politics, stays true to the new science of the Earth System.[32])

The view that the new epoch is just another name for human disturbance to the environment has recently been reprised by law professor Jedediah Purdy in a "death-of-nature" tome that seems to have been written without reading *any* scientific papers on the topic at all, instead preferring to find the evidence for the new geological epoch in Thoreau's 1854 transcendentalist classic *Walden*. And so Purdy can begin with the dispiritingly postmodern claim that the idea of the Anthropocene "despite its scientific trappings" is really a "cultural idea,"[33] before devoting the rest of the book to "a history of how Americans have shaped their landscape" and the ideas it gave rise to. In other words, he constructs a history of the new epoch before the new epoch actually began.

The essential failing is that the paradigm shift of Earth System science is not recognized, and so some scientists read the Anthropocene into the old disciplines with which they are comfortable. It is not that the old disciplines have been disproved or even made redundant when applied to the old objects, such as the landscape, ecosystems, and the environment. A new object has appeared, the Earth System. Its arrival gave rise to the new paradigm of Earth System science, and the new science shaped our understanding of the new object. While recognized by Earth System scientists and a few pioneers in science studies, others treat the Earth System and so the Anthropocene as if it were a further articulation of the old object (landscapes or ecosystems) and its study the continued development of established environmental sciences. So, unlike the "typical" scientific revolution, it has not been the case that the new evidence contradicts the prevailing theory, but that the focus of interest shifted due to the appearance of new phenomena – Earth System processes that transcend the bounds of ecosystems and operate at a global level. These new phenomena required a new object. For this, new concepts were needed.

As I have suggested, beyond its scientific importance, the appearance of this new object, the Earth System, has ontological meaning. It invites us to think about the Earth in a new way, an Earth in which it is possible for humankind to participate directly in its evolution by influencing the constantly changing processes that constitute it. It therefore brings out the conception of a joint human–Earth story, one explored later in this book.

The ecomodernist gloss

Most who read the Earth System scientists' papers on the Anthropocene – and especially the projections of climate scientists – understand the new epoch as a consequence of the industrial growth process whose harms will range from severe to calamitous. Severe harms are evident already. However, a rising chorus of writers and intellectuals actually *welcomes* its arrival, expressing a certain excitement or exhilaration. At the entrance to the first major scientific conference devoted to the new epoch in 2012, a huge sign proclaimed "Welcome to the Anthropocene." I interpreted the slogan as ironic. It was only over the next two or three years that I realized it was not dark humour but a true expression of the sentiment of those who see disturbance of the Earth System as a wonderful opportunity for humankind to prove our ingenuity and technological faculty.

Perhaps the excitement is a reaction to postmodern anomie, to the essential boredom and hollowness of modern life in affluent countries or, among intellectuals, a restless desire in an era of stifling intellectual orthodoxy, where nothing big happens or seems possible, to go somewhere risky whatever the moral cost. Like soldiers marching off to World War I, these influential voices embrace the prospect of leaving the safety of their Holocene home and embarking on the foreign adventure of the Anthropocene.

This kind of scientific adventurism seems to underlie the collaboration known as Future Earth, which foresees a sustainable and equitable world in which we may all thrive. Some leading geoengineering researchers are enthusiastic at the prospect of humans assuming control of the planet. David Keith is perhaps the foremost scientific advocate of solar geoengineering, that is, coating the Earth with a layer of sulphate particles in the upper atmosphere to reduce the amount of sunlight reaching the planet. He writes of his "delight" in humankind's "new powers to shape the planetary environment," hoping we will use them to "build a thriving civilization."[34]

The most prominent among those who view the Anthropocene as an event to be celebrated rather than lamented or feared are those environmentalists, concentrated in the United States, who brand themselves "ecomodernists." It is worth dwelling on their worldview because they may be seen as the most articulate representatives of the dominant economic-political system. If those at the pinnacle of corporate and political power – meeting perhaps at Davos – were to express a view of the Anthropocene, they would take their cue from them. (John Bellamy Foster and colleagues see ecomodernists as the most apologetic strand of the social sciences. Their political quiescence and faith in the prevailing system seems to deepen as the natural scientists become more alarmed.[35])

For the ecomodernists, instead of final proof of the dangers of hubris, the new epoch is greeted as a sign of humankind's ability to renovate and control nature. They take to heart the observation, made by Isabella in Shakespeare's *Measure for Measure*, that "It is excellent to have a giant's strength" without noticing the caveat, "but it is tyrannous to use it like a giant." And so in this eco-Promethean view, the Anthropocene is not evidence of human short-sightedness or foolishness, nor of global capitalism's rapaciousness, but presents an opportunity for humans finally to come into their own. Several years ago they began to speak of the *good* Anthropocene: there are no planetary boundaries that limit continued growth in human populations and economic advance because "human systems" can adapt and indeed prosper in a warming world. History proves our flexibility and the Anthropocene is another challenge for us to overcome.

In this view, as we enter the Anthropocene we should not fear transgressing natural limits; the only barrier to a grand new era for humanity is our own self-doubt. Recapitulating Francis Bacon's 1627 vision of *New Atlantis* in which science and technology become the foundations of a Utopia, leading ecomodernist Erle Ellis urges us to see the Anthropocene not as a crisis but as "the beginning of a new geological epoch ripe with human-directed opportunity."[36] Romantic critics of technology, and the gloomy scientists they draw on, stand in the way of the vision's realization. Humanity's transition to a higher level of planetary significance is "an amazing opportunity" and "we will be proud of the planet we create in the Anthropocene."[37] Coordinated and promoted by the Breakthrough Institute, the San Francisco think tank that forms the institutional heart of ecomodernism, the vision has been condensed into *An Ecomodernist Manifesto* in which signatories transcend the modest aim of a *good* Anthropocene to envision a "*great* Anthropocene."

For the ecomodernists, if we are capable of developing technologies to control the climate and regulate the Earth as a whole, then why not? Planetary engineering reframes global warming. No longer a vindication of environmentalist warnings that humans have gone too far, climate change becomes the spur to final victory for the human mastery project. Just as Francis Bacon understood Nature as a passive entity to be manipulated once her secrets had been extracted (by putting her "on the rack" if necessary) and saw the exercise of human creative power facing no constraints, so the ecomoderns understand the Earth as a system that can be subdued with knowledge and technological power. And so the idea of engineering the climate system is attracting the support of conservative political actors, including think tanks with histories of climate science denial.[38]

Some might admire the ecomodernists' audacious claim to

human omniscience and omnipotence, and the adroitness with which they turn the negative consequences of the growth project into a new and higher form of positivity. As humanists with a Whig view of history (history as the inevitable rise of liberty and enlightenment), the ecomodernists claim to found the good Anthropocene argument on science rather than faith or politics. In this respect it can be shown that their vision of the future is based on misconstrued science. Peter Kareiva and colleagues express their central scientific claim: "Nature is so resilient that it can recover rapidly from even the most powerful human disturbances."[39] The belief that ecosystems can "bounce back" is carried over to their interpretation of the Anthropocene. Ellis puts it plainly: "Humans have dramatically altered natural systems … and yet the Earth has become more productive and more capable of supporting the human population. … *there is little evidence to date that this dynamic has been fundamentally altered*."[40]

In fact, the essential insight of the most eminent Earth System scientists is exactly the reverse – the dynamic between humans and the Earth *has* been fundamentally altered, because there has been a phase shift in the functioning of the Earth System as a whole. We have, as a number of leading Earth System researchers put it, entered a "*no-analogue state*" – the Earth has never been here before. The Holocene conditions that provide the platform for the idea of the "good Anthropocene" have been relegated to the past because the system's operation has been disrupted. Whatever its validity in the Holocene, the argument that ecosystems are resilient and can "bounce back" from human disturbance is simply not relevant to shifts in geochronology.

Throughout the late eighteenth and nineteenth centuries the

new science of geology was dominated by uniformitarianism, the idea that the Earth is shaped by slow-moving forces that gradually transform it over very long time periods. Determined to distance the new science from biblical accounts of instantaneous creation and divinely sent floods, the emerging profession was reluctant to accept any theory of catastrophism in which a transition from one period in Earth history to the next may be due to some natural paroxysm. In the end, the evidence for catastrophic changes (due, for example, to asteroid strikes) could no longer be resisted and geologists accepted that gradual change can at times be interrupted by cataclysms. Today the Geological Time Scale includes several transitions from one era or epoch to the next caused by catastrophic events, ones so rapid that most existing life forms cannot adapt and die out.

Geologically speaking, the Anthropocene event, occurring over an extremely short period, is an instance of catastrophism, so that the ecomodernists' conception of the Earth as resilient and able to bounce back from even large disturbances is a uniformitarian understanding. The "good Anthropocene" is therefore an anachronism in the precise sense. The ecomodernists' belief in gradual change in Earth history echoes their commitment to gradual social change. Both science and politics are construed in ways supportive of the prevailing system; both ecosystems and American society have proven themselves to be adaptable and resilient, and combine to deliver stability and prosperity. Human ingenuity and technological solutions have fixed glitches in both systems in the past and will do so in the future.

It's worth noting for later that if the ecomodernists are successors to Bacon in their commitment to a "second creation" by technological means, they do not share the Baconian presupposition that the ability to remake nature is a divine gift. So, if not from God, from where does the authority derive to master the Earth? The ecomodernists argue as secular humanists: the authority to take control of nature is self-granted, a power ceded to humans for the first time by Enlightenment philosophy.

I hope it is by now apparent just how vital it is to recognize that the Anthropocene is a very recent *rupture* in Earth history and so in human history.

An epoch by any other name

In the debate among social scientists and humanities scholars over the Anthropocene, no aspect of it has attracted more ire than the term itself. Dozens of papers, books, and commentaries have been devoted to attacking the meaning and implications of assigning the new epoch to humanity in general, to an undifferentiated *anthropos*. There are two linked anxieties. First, the term "Anthropocene" distributes responsibility to everyone and away from those actually answerable for bringing on the new epoch, the nations of the North and especially those in control of the economic-political system. As a result, the Anthropocene concept risks, in the words of its critics, "serving as a legitimizing philosophy for an oligarchic geopower."[41]

Second, even if all humans were responsible, by locating the cause in the activities of "abstract humanity" we inevitably shift from actual history into "species thinking," that is, thinking in terms of the imagined universal qualities of the human species, instead of evolving social, economic, and political structures, and in particular the history of capitalism. The term implies a narrative of humans-as-a-whole rising to planetary supremacy, so that the new epoch, the Anthropocene, emerges out of the nature of the species as such.[42] I will consider this second anxiety in chapter 2.

One of the implications of the attack on the term is that Earth System scientists – in particular the Nobel Prize-winning atmospheric chemist Paul Crutzen who first blurted it out – made a mistake and should have understood the political implications of what they were doing. A Marxist critic, Jason Moore, suggests they should have been more sensitive to the "actually existing" historical relations in choosing an appropriate name, rather than one that results in "the erasure of capitalism's historical specificity."[43] He replaces the scientists' flawed neologism with his own, the "Capitalocene," as if the naming of geological divisions belonged to sociology.

In my view, while the basic point is worth making, the outrage over Crutzen's coinage has been a distraction from deeper questions. In the first place, the term "Anthropocene" is here to stay. Social scientists are free to comment on the implications of a name, and it is their role to analyze the forces that brought about the new epoch; but it is the scientists addressing the International Commission on Stratigraphy whose role it is to name divisions in the Geological Time Scale, including the Holocene's successor. Earth System scientists are scientists, so we would expect them to choose a "politically neutral" term. (Yes, it only *seems* politically neutral.) Moreover, some of those at the center of Anthropocene science are fully aware of the roots of the new epoch in capitalist industrialization in Europe and its extraordinary post-war acceleration due to rampant consumerism and the power of the fossil-fuel lobby. They are also apprised, because they study the regional statistics, of the profoundly unequal distribution of causes and impacts, although it is true that some make gratuitous declarations about what should be done. Paul Crutzen has rightly been chastised for suggesting at the end of one of his seminal pieces that the answers to the Anthropocene are to be found in science and engineering, including geoengineering.[44]

The angst over the term reflects the continuing influence of the "semiotic turn" in the social sciences and humanities, and its emphasis on the power of language. Yes, words matter; but there are forces much more powerful than words, and to excoriate scientists for terminological naivety exaggerates the importance of the choice of the name for a new division in the Geological Time Scale in a way that implicitly supplants the prerogative of Earth science to name epochs with the claims of certain social sciences. In doing so, the latter are stating that the Anthropocene idea is only another way of capturing what we have been saying for a long time. Only those who have not yet grasped that a *rupture* has occurred in the social world as well as the physical one can see it this way.

Some historians want to reclaim the new geological epoch for their discipline, complaining that today "it is the sciences of the Earth system, and no longer historians, who name the epoch in which we are living."[45] This must be an epistemological mistake; the Anthropocene describes a *geological* epoch and not a social-historical one. If geological history and human history have "converged," then it does not mean that geology has become social science. Historical epochs will map onto recent geological history in varying ways, and the new geological epoch will influence how we think about history. But merging geochronology with human history leads down a path in which changes to the functioning of the Earth System must be explained as changes in social relations. Of course we can understand the Industrial Revolution as the outgrowth of earlier transformations – of mercantile capitalism, colonialism, and transatlantic trade – but to suggest (as Moore does) that the Anthropocene therefore began in the sixteenth century, even though there were no detectable signs of disturbance to the Earth System until the nineteenth century, is to discount scientific facts altogether, which suggests something disquieting about the evolution of the humanities and social sciences. Moore takes this tendency to a risible extreme when he condemns the Anthropocene's "fundamentally bourgeois character."[46]

Beyond all of the arguments above, there is a more pragmatic reason for attaching the new epoch to an undifferentiated *anthropos*. If the preponderance of blame once lay with Europe and America, it no longer does. Focusing only on climate change (though the same applies to other human contributors to Earth System disturbance), China's 1.4 billion people now have around the same *average* carbon emissions as Europeans. China's annual greenhouse gas emissions now easily exceed those of the United States, and China's total historical emissions will soon be larger than those of the United States. With India's 1.3 billion people next in line (the two account for almost 40 percent of the world's population), by the middle of the century the South will be responsible, both contemporaneously and historically, for much more damage to the global climate system than the North as it copies the northern model of environmental harm in the pursuit of poverty-alleviation and affluence. By 2050 at the latest the objections to

"Anthropocene" will seem very dated. If the "Anthropocene" was a Eurocentric idea when it was coined, it is now Sino-Americo-Eurocentric, and in a decade or two it will be Indo-Sino-Americo-Eurocentric.

None of this exonerates the North from its historical responsibility and its shameful reluctance to respond to the danger once it became undeniable. Even so, it must be accepted that the old world of North and South is vanishing. "Aha," some will reply, "but China's emissions do not count because a large portion of them is emitted making consumer goods exported to the North." The intention of this argument is to keep China firmly in the exploited South by continuing to attribute sole blame for climate change to the North and the capitalist world-system it established and still enforces. Yet the example of China shows it's time to abandon this "dependency theory" developed in the 1960s and 1970s to explain continued subservience of the South after decolonization, and later elaborated into world-system analysis (according to which the globe is organized around an international division of labor and capital in which the "core" of rich countries exploits the "periphery" of poor ones). For a start, the share of China's emissions arising from export manufacture has been around 30 percent, but it is declining as China reorients its economy toward domestic consumption, which year on year erodes the basis of the argument. Moreover, China *chose* the path of export-oriented industrialization as an act of pure national sovereignty and it did so as the quickest way of enriching itself. Corporations in the North did not force their dirty factories on China; China chose to allow them in as a means of soaking up its low-cost labor. Foreign corporations, even the most powerful ones, often found themselves at the mercy of hard-nosed domestic players. In addition, the United States has funded much of its public debt by borrowing from China's central bank, and in 2008 found that its ability to respond to the financial crisis was severely constrained by its indebtedness to China. To characterize China's astonishing economic growth rates in the 1990s and 2000s, and so its enormous greenhouse gas emissions, as the result of neo-colonial manipulation puts radical critique before actual history.

As an aside, there were historical precedents for nations of the South asserting their sovereignty. In the 1960s, South Korea successfully pursued a sovereign path of export-oriented industrialization and modernization in order to overcome its own "backwardness."[47] The economic strategy was not imposed on it by the United States (which had a great deal of influence after the Korean War). Nor was Korea forced to take the rich nations' dirty industries. The Korean state actively set out to take them. In fact, under military strongman President Park Chung-hee, Korea explicitly rejected the urging of the United States and the precursor of the World Bank to pursue exports of traditional commodities (rice and silk) and instead invested in state-sponsored, export-oriented manufacturing industries. To put the decision into effect, President Park called in the most powerful members of the mercantile class and told them that unless they took their capital out of trading enterprises and invested it in manufacturing he would throw them in jail. Korea was no client state.

So, far from being a product of "unequal relations of power, exchange and distribution in world society,"[48] China's massive greenhouse gas emissions are an expression of its sovereign power. If anything, compared to the United States, and certainly to

Europe, global power and economic strength has tilted in China's favor, as will be attested to by many in Africa, where Chinese corporations have bought up huge swathes of land and resources. China's coal-fueled growth has given it *too much* power over others. Attempts to keep China in the exploited South confront these incontestable facts. The widening split within the South at international climate change negotiations has been apparent for some time. At the Copenhagen climate change conference in 2009, China effectively abandoned the small-island states and the most vulnerable countries to ruthlessly pursue its own economic and geopolitical interests. The understanding of the globe that emerged in the 1950s and 1960s as one divided between North and South has been overturned by history, and the *rupture* of the Anthropocene arrives to challenge social science to build new theories.

If these arguments fail to convince the reader that China itself is responsible for the environmental damage caused by its industrialization, perhaps a last one will. If China's emissions generated by manufacturing exports are to be discounted because consumers in the North benefit from them, what are we to do with emissions generated in Australia in the production of iron ore, nickel, alumina, and coal destined for export? Should the consumers of these resources in India and China be responsible for the emissions in Australia? Of course not. In fact, many believe that Australia should take responsibility not only for the emissions in Australia from mining and transporting coal but for the emissions from burning that coal, even though they occur in other countries.

As each year passes, responsibility for anthropogenic climate change shifts from the North to the South, where "responsibility"

is measured not only in the international greenhouse gas accounting system but also in the moral accounts (whose ledgers are locked
away in the historical memory). Although there is some distance
still to travel, like the North the large industrializing nations of the
South increasingly have the ability to choose to do otherwise – and
some do, led by China itself. If with his neologism Paul Crutzen is
guilty of implicitly blaming humanity in general for the sins of the
North, he can be accused at worst of being two or three decades
premature. It's true, and vital to understand, that the model of
capitalist modernization pursued by China, India, and other
nations of the South is thoroughly European in origin. Yet, if the
anthropos of "the Anthropocene" conceals its European pedigree,
we may today speak of an *anthropos* with Chinese characteristics.

Although I have focused on practical defenses of the deployment of an undifferentiated *anthropos* to designate the new epoch
there is a deeper reason, one I flag here and develop throughout
the book. If the Anthropocene concept emerged from the new
discipline of Earth System science, its core insight was to conceive of the Earth no longer as a collection of ecosystems, landscapes, catchments, and so on, but as a single, total functioning
system. From an Earth System viewpoint, there are on Earth no
divisions between North and South or between nations, cultures,
genders, and races. There are only humans with more or less power
to disturb it. If the Anthropocene is a rupture in the history of the
Earth as a whole, then it is also a rupture in the history of humans
as a whole.

It goes without saying that beginning with *divisions* among
humans is indispensable for understanding all kinds of problems
in the world, just as fixing on ecosystems rather than the Earth

System as a whole is the only way to answer certain kinds of environmental questions. "That is all very well," the skeptical reader may be asking, "but if the Earth System recognizes only humans-in-general what exactly are these beings?" Clearly, the modern conception of the human that grew out of the Enlightenment will no longer do and in what follows I hope to provide some suggestions as to how we might formulate an answer to the epochal question: what is this being who has changed the course of the Earth itself?

2 A New Anthropocentrism

To doubt everything

When discussion turns to the Anthropocene's reconfiguration of humankind's relationship with the Earth it is sometimes met with "Well, those ideas do not resonate with me" or "They are not part of my cultural background." There was a time, in the seventeenth and eighteenth centuries, when the idea of mechanical nature operating according to knowable physical laws did not resonate in the ears of most of those who heard them for the first time. A mechanical universe went against the grain of their comprehension of the world around them; the rupture of modernity was deeply discomforting. In the same way, the Anthropocene's advent brings a break in thinking commensurate with the break in the Earth's functioning because it contradicts the understanding of the world brought by modernity three or four centuries ago. So what is it about the Anthropocene that qualifies its arrival as a historical *breach* of comparable magnitude, one that demands we set aside our accustomed understanding and reconsider everything?

First, we face the real prospect that over this century humans will, in full knowledge of what we are doing, irreparably degrade the conditions of life on our home planet. Second, we must concede the material possibility of our own extinction, or at least the collapse of civilized ways of life, as a result of our own actions. Third, the functioning of the Earth has changed. No longer governed solely by blind forces, its progress is now influenced by the injection of an ontologically distinct force of nature, one that expresses human will. The globe is no longer the "disenchanted" Earth given to us by the scientific revolution. But nor is it "re-enchanted"; it is not magic that pervades it but willed activity. In addition, the pleasant and predictable climate of the Holocene epoch, which was the environmental context for the emergence of civilization and the cultures and social structures that accompanied it, has been relegated to the past; we are entering a new, unstable, and unpredictable geological era that will endure for thousands or tens of thousands of years.

In short, the relationship of human beings to the natural world we inhabit has been upended. None of this could have been foreseen a century ago, or even three decades ago. Yet now we must face up to the fact that this situation, an irreversible and dangerous shift in the Earth's trajectory, is our future and the ideas that we have inherited from the era before the break must all be open to question. Among many that I will later challenge, one is worth mentioning here. It appears that the wanton use of our freedom and technological power have led us to the brink of ruin. The very cultivation of our powers has left us exposed to a nature that refuses to be tamed and is increasingly unsympathetic to our interests.

In the face of the Anthropocene rent in the fabric of the world, we are obliged to doubt all of our beliefs. When a new idea comes along that encapsulates a new dispensation it is simply untenable to declare that it "does not resonate with my view of the world," because it is precisely your view of the world that may no longer provide a reliable guide to thinking. In the current circumstances, to declare "I don't like the sound of this new idea" may be to declare "I refuse to accept that the world has changed." The rupture challenges our conceptions no matter which culture they are embedded in. Appealing to one's particular culture or religion – in short, tradition – is no argument because belonging to a certain cultural or religious group does not exempt one from what is happening on Anthropocene Earth. There are no more enclaves.

The natural world inherited by modernity is gone, and all of the ideas built on it now float on its memory. In that view, over and against nature as the passive repository of resources and "values" of various kinds, operating according to knowable laws working themselves out blindly, stood humans, who strove to detach themselves from it. Even if we do not yet possess a coherent alternative conception, it is apparent that this modern world-picture is no longer tenable; it is contradicted by the facts. So we are faced with the discomforting choice between groping unsteadily toward new conceptions that attempt to build on the new real, or clinging to old conceptions rooted in a world that has been left behind. Retreating to tradition will not do, except insofar as we can find in tradition resources that help us comprehend and respond to what none of them could have foreseen. A sensibility of human folly and vulnerability would be a helpful start.

Against the new real of the Anthropocene, we can find those

who do not believe we can ever have the power to change the future of the Earth (deniers and some religious fundamentalists), those who want us to relinquish the capacity (deep greens and ecocentric philosophers), those who accept we have the power and argue we should not be afraid to exercise it (ecomoderns), and those who are oblivious and forge ahead regardless of any consequence (the avatars of the ruling system and its intellectual apologists). And then there are those who accept we have the power but must fear its misuse, believing we have used it recklessly and must pull back and deploy it much more judiciously and respectfully. It is the latter that gives rise to what I will call "the new anthropocentrism."

Anthropocentrism redux

In recent times scholars and activists have labored to persuade us that the belief that the human is a unique creature with special powers and responsibilities is a conceit. It is pointed out that we share 98.8 percent of our DNA with chimpanzees. Instead of taking this factoid as a measure of the meaninglessness of crude genetic tallies, it is read as if we are virtually identical to our simian cousins. Psychologists and ethologists have worked hard to show that some animals have the ability to use and even to fashion tools, that they have languages, that they can solve cognitive problems and possess memories, and that they have emotions and interior lives similar to those of humans. Others turn to philosophical arguments to make the case that sentient beings ought to have the same rights as humans.

Although these attempts to cut humans down to size are well motivated, aimed as they often have been at countering the unending violence committed against other creatures by humans inured to the suffering of others or possessed by a sense of species entitlement, there is something desperate about arguments that equate human beings with chimps, dolphins, and dogs when on any measure the unbridgeable gulf between humans and the rest of creation is blindingly apparent. When we consider, if only for a moment, the vast scale of human achievement – writing, cities, mathematics, agriculture, medicine, splitting the atom, space travel, literature, and art galleries, not to mention theorizing about our equality with animals – the rudimentary tools, "language," and cultural products of the animal kingdom pale into insignificance.

It may seem harsh to state these facts so bluntly. The intention is not to deny that humans are responsible for subjecting animals to unconscionable suffering, or that certain other creatures – elephants, dolphins, great apes – possess much greater intelligence and deeper, more complex inner lives than we have given them credit for. Yet these facts only point to the shock and pain those creatures perhaps feel as they witness the devastation wrought on them by this marauding creature known as human. Reaffirming these facts does not carry the imputation that other animals are "sub-human," except for those who believe animals are rightly judged by the extent to which they mirror human capacities. The worth of other beings ought not to depend on their skills, and it is by sweeping away attempts to show that some animals are really like us that we can accept and admire their own innate integrity as living beings. Nevertheless, whatever one believes philosophically – whether one keeps them in incommensurable categories or believes that animals can be elevated to human status – none of it changes the essential fact of the Anthropocene.

What is new, and will prompt me to argue for a *new anthropocentrism*, is the arrival of a geological epoch in which humans now rival the great forces of nature. The future of the entire planet, including many forms of life, is now contingent on the decisions of a conscious force, even if the signs of it acting in concert are only embryonic (and may be still-born). In the face of this brute fact, the defining truth of the age, denying the uniqueness and power of humans becomes perverse. Every scientific study that corroborates human disturbance of the Earth System confirms the truth of our special place on the planet. Whatever the political attractions of various critiques of humankind's central agency, the Anthropocene arrives to blow them all away and instantiate humankind once and for all as the being at the center of the Earth. As each year passes, the chasm between human beings and every other creature only widens.

However, *it is vital to recognize* that the relationship of humans to other creatures is not the same as the relationship of humans to the Earth as a whole. Collapsing other creatures, their environments, and the Earth System into "nature" only brings confusion. From Earth System science it ought to be apparent by now that humans can *never* master the Earth; its power is too great and will always prevail, whatever local "victories" humans may have. If in the Anthropocene the "giant has been wakened" and is flexing its muscles, the continued belief that we can master such a fractious and uncontainable beast becomes not mere hubris but crazy-brave. Even so, compared to all other creatures humans stand out, the creature whose capacities and achievements set it apart. Humans are the dominant animal, with dominion over others, a truth confirmed by the astounding calculations of Vaclav Smil.[1]

If we were to divide all terrestrial vertebrates on Earth into the three classes of wild animals, domesticated animals, and human beings, and weighed them to obtain their total mass, then it turns out that humans account for 30 percent of the total mass of all animals on Earth and animals domesticated for human use account for 67 percent. That leaves all of the wild animals on the Earth's surface accounting for no more than 3 percent.

These numbers alone testify to the power this special creature has accumulated in recent times, confirming its status as the central agent on the Earth as a whole. It ought to be stressed, though, that the *responsibility* humans have for the creatures we dominate is not the same kind of responsibility we have not to disrupt the functioning of the Earth System, which we can never dominate. The responsibility to protect is a different kind of moral duty from the responsibility to placate.

Anthropocentrism – less a philosophy than a philosophical and practical presupposition – has a complex history, not least because it depends on diverging understandings of the "nature" humans are thought to be at the center of. I will comment on anthropocentrisms presently, and the decisive philosophical implications of the shift from "nature" to "Earth System." If it's true that our ecological predicament has come about because of our anthropocentrism, then the answer seems to be to replace a human-centered understanding of the world with a biocentric or ecocentric standpoint or one with no center. Yet is not the essential lesson of Anthropocene science that it's too late for us to abandon an anthropocentric standpoint, even if it were possible to do so?

We can no longer withdraw and expect nature to return to any kind of "natural" state. There is no going back to the Holocene. We may have acquired it foolishly, but we now have a responsibility for the Earth as a whole and pretending otherwise is itself irresponsible. So the question is not whether human beings stand at the center of the world, but what *kind* of human being stands at the center of the world, and what is the nature of that world.

Let me be very clear here. I am insisting that a sharp division must be made between anthropocentrism as a scientific fact – humans *are* the dominant creature, so dominant that we have shifted the geological arc of the planet – and anthropocentrism as a normative claim: that it is right and proper that humans should be masters of the Earth. Never has the "is" been more apparent; never has the "ought" been less defensible. The constant elision of the two, the confusion of the "is" with the "ought," has led many who should know better to renounce the actual; those who rebel most strongly against the normative claim of domination feel they must reject the scientific fact of it. I will return to the lamentable consequences of this mix-up.

The original fault in the growth-driven techno-industrial system is its *monstrous* anthropocentrism rather than its anthropocentrism as such. The problem is not that humans are anthropocentric, but that *we are not anthropocentric enough*. This might sound like the kind of transgressive statement concocted to startle but which with repeated use feels like an authorial ploy. But it is in fact the essential claim of this book: we refuse to face up to the profound importance of humans, ontologically and now practically, to the Earth and its future. Instead of accepting responsibility for the power we possess, we continue to exercise it rashly

43

as if nothing else mattered. Of course, this entrenched form of anthropocentrism is a kind of disavowal, reveling in an *anthropos* with no higher meaning, no responsibility, and no ontological uniqueness, an adolescent immersion in appetites without the adult understanding of the obligation that goes with the power to satisfy them.

The error of monstrous anthropocentrism is not that it recognizes humans as the exceptional creature – for that is now indisputable – but that it elevates the human to an exalted place of power-without-responsibility in a way that denies or is blind to the true burden that humans carry, a burden now overwhelming us with the Anthropocene's arrival.

Any defense of anthropocentrism naturally creates anxiety. Does not the elevation of humans to the status of the special creature inevitably bring hubris? In other words, if we admit anthropocentrism we cannot avoid anthropo-supremacism. In truth, we have no choice other than to insist on a distinction between an arrogant anthropocentrism and a humble anthropocentrism. To be humble does not require that we deny our significance; indeed, the greatest humility is available to the most significant. Fêted by Hollywood and pursued by world leaders, the Dalai Lama has far greater opportunity for self-effacement than any one of his multitude of anonymous devotees. For humankind as a whole it was easy to be humble before nature prior to the invention of the steam engine, let alone the nuclear reactor. But one cannot deny that, whether we like it or not, techno-industrial growth *has* placed humans in a position of power. Some refuse to believe that we have assumed this place; the question, however, is no longer whether we accept the role, but how we exercise it.

The antinomy of the Anthropocene

The reader may have noticed an apparent contradiction between the two essential claims made so far. On the one hand, the science tells us that humans have become so powerful that we rival the great forces of nature, to the point where we have altered the trajectory of the planet. On the other hand, the forces of nature have been roused from their Holocene slumber so that we enter a long era in which they are more dangerous to us and more uncontrollable. Humans have never been more potent and have never exercised more domination over nature, yet we are now vulnerable to the power of nature in a way we have not known for at least 10,000 years since the last great ice-sheets finally retreated, opening up vast swathes of temperate land suitable for the flourishing of human populations. The climate system is becoming more energetic, bringing more storms, wildfires, droughts, and heatwaves. So, while technology allows us to divert rivers and harness the power of the atom, "Gaia has been enraged" and sends extreme events before which our powers appear puny. Just as technology has put enormous new influence in the hands of the dominant creature, nature's dormant powers have been unleashed, making them less predictable, more dangerous, and, crucially, less subject to human control.

Humans are more powerful; nature is more powerful. Taken together, there is more power at work on Earth. A power struggle between humankind and Earth is under way, a tug-of-war in which humans strain to drag the Earth into our sphere of influence while Earth attempts to pull us back into its domain. If the Moderns understood the tug-of-war as the task of hauling a heavy, inert object into their domain using ever-more effective techniques, they have yet to realize that the object is now pulling back, and doing so with ever-greater force. As we will see, some philosophical stances recognize only the increased power of the Earth, some only the increased power of humans, while others recognize neither. Only when we accept both can we properly grasp the new situation humans confront. In the next chapter I will use this schema to assess various philosophical understandings of the Anthropocene.

Some Prometheans, the geoengineers, are convinced that humans can use their technological might to subdue the restless forces of the Earth System. Yet the unleashing of the Earth's powers has barely begun. Humans may or may not yet have pushed the system beyond the major tipping points that would trigger unstoppable feedback processes, including a melting West Antarctic ice-sheet, thawing Siberian permafrost, and dieback of Amazon rainforests, although perusal of the latest studies suggest we inevitably will. When that point of no return is crossed, if it has not been already, we will face a different kind of Earth, one that will increasingly render humans and their technologies feeble by comparison. At some far distant point in the future, after a life-or-death lottery for the Earth's biological inhabitants, the Earth System will settle into a new equilibrium. The new "basin of attraction" will be marked by little or no polar ice, a world congenial for insects and reptiles but inhospitable for large mammals like us.[2] Keeping alive the sense of human invulnerability accumulated during the last two or three centuries of the Holocene grows more willful by the day.

Our understanding of the Earth we inhabit is undergoing a radical change. The modern ideas of the Earth as the environment in which humans make their home, or as a knowable collection of ecosystems more or less disturbed by humans, is being replaced by the conception of an inscrutable and unpredictable entity with a violent history and volatile "mood swings." Earth System scientists have reached for rough metaphors to capture this new idea – images of "the wakened giant" and "the ornery beast," of Gaia "fighting back" and seeking "revenge," a world of "angry summers" and "death spirals."

This new conception of the Earth System is inconsistent with the understanding of a nature victimized and colonized by humans that has emerged since the 1960s. It is an understanding captured in phrases from the 1990s like "the end of nature," "nothing but us" and "the Earth's cry for rescue," and morphing into more recent renderings like "a humanized Earth," "the kind of nature we wish to have," "Nature no longer exists apart from humanity," and "It is our choice what happens here." Whether the mood is one of lament or triumph, in all of these expressions nature is our victim or servant.

Yet Earth System science now tells us that, rather than dying, nature as the Earth System has in fact *come alive* or (perhaps a better metaphor) is waking from its slumber. It's true that wherever we look we see human influence, but at the same time we see stirring an "angry," "ornery," "vengeful" Earth that is more *detached* from us than it has been for 10,000 years. Contrary to the comforting expectation that in the Anthropocene we can have "the kind of nature we wish to have," as we enter the new epoch we will meet an Earth that is further and further from the Earth we might want. And against the belief that "the world we will inhabit is the one we have made,"[3] the world we will have to live with is the Earth we have turned against us.

In other words, these views of the end of nature and a humanized Earth subject to our choices may have been appropriate to the Holocene, but Holocene thinking has been supplanted by Anthropocene thinking. This all follows from the primary fact that the Anthropocene is a *rupture*, whereas all of these views about the death of nature and so on do not recognize that a rupture has occurred but write as if there is continuity, a continuous process of human colonization going back thousands of years, albeit one that has intensified in recent decades.

So on this new Earth, notions of human domination – whether positively as mastery or negatively as victimization – have to be discarded. It follows that the benign ideas of good stewardship and a loving Mother Earth are redundant too. Nature is no longer passive and fragile, suffering in silence, "the sister who cries out to us," in the words of Pope Francis. In the Anthropocene, it is no longer tenable to believe that "our common home is like a sister with whom we share our life and a beautiful mother who opens her arms to embrace us."[4] In the Holocene, to view the world, as the encyclical does, as "entrusted to men and women" was a plausible working hypothesis. But no more. Now, when Mother Earth opens her arms it is not to embrace but to crush us. Our goal can no longer be to "save nature" but to save ourselves, from ourselves and from nature, knowing that every disturbance to the Earth System reduces the chances of doing so. Nature is no longer (as Pope Francis writes) "a magnificent book in which God speaks to us and grants us a glimpse of his infinite beauty and goodness," but a grim report in which scientists speak to us and grant us a glimpse of disrupted natural patterns and a chaotic climate. Or perhaps it is more accurate to say that it is both, *a sublime Earth* that presents itself to us as beautiful when becalmed and terrifying when enraged, an intimate planet and an alien one, Mother and Other.

In previous times, human aspirations were often tempered by a belief in an all-powerful deity. If today the Almighty no longer restrains us there is a more palpable force that stands in the way of any ambition we may have for total control, and that is the Earth itself. This epoch-marking fact reframes all anthropocentric claims; but it does so not by displacing the center of the world to somewhere else, not by denying our extraordinary power, and not by repudiating our decisive role in planetary history.

The competing forces of the power of humans to disrupt the Earth System and the uncontrollable powers of nature unleashed in the Anthropocene give rise to what I call "the new anthropocentrism." I will argue that humankind became a unified entity – the *anthropos* – for the first time only in the second half of the twentieth century, and as such has become *the central agent on a new kind of Earth*, one delimited by the newly activated and countervailing power of the Earth System. The philosophical anthropocentrism I develop diverges from the anthropo-supremacism that brought us the ecological crisis; yet it also runs contrary to virtually all philosophical understandings of modern environmentalism and post-humanism. Attempts to counter anthropocentric stances by adopting a non-human-centered standpoint (that of nature, or ecosystems, or other creatures), or by spreading agency around without regard to the human exception, cannot resist the evidence of Earth System science.

If the old anthropocentrism can be visualized as a world revolving round humans, there is no easy way to picture the new anthropocentrism. The cosmological phenomenon of double planets is suggestive – two planets of approximately equal size with a common center of gravity rotating round each other.[5] Planet Human and Planet Earth are co-orbitally bound together so that "the fate of one determines the fate of the other." Standing on Planet Human, it appears that Planet Earth revolves round Planet Human. But if we place ourselves on Planet Earth, it is apparent that Planet Human orbits Planet Earth. If either planet were to disappear the other would fly off into the nothingness of space, despite those who insist that Earth is indifferent to the elimination of humans. (I make the case for the significance of humans in chapter 4.)

The new anthropocentrism

The new anthropocentrism of the Anthropocene follows from our emerging understanding of the Earth System and humankind's role in it. The case can be brought together as follows.

1. Instead of old ideas of nature, we inhabit the Earth System, that is, the planet, taken as a whole, in a constant state of movement, driven by interconnected cycles and forces, from its core out to the atmosphere and beyond to the Moon, and powered by the flow of energy from the Sun.
2. Human activity participates in and modifies many of the myriad processes that constitute the Earth System, as well as the ecosystems within it.

3.) Human activity has modified the Earth's processes so radically that we have disrupted the great forces of nature governing the Earth System's evolution, so much so that it has shifted into a new geological epoch.

4.) We do not have dominion over the Earth and it is folly to attempt to exert control over the Earth System (by way of planetary-scale geoengineering, for example). Yet it is too late to pull back and hope that everything would revert to a pre-disrupted state. Some of the disruptions we have caused to Earth System processes are now irreversible and the effects will persist for millennia. It is too late to go back to the Holocene.

5.) When the above facts have been absorbed, the questions facing humankind become: what can be done to slow the changes; what can be done to adapt to those that are unavoidable; and, over the long term, what can be done to remediate the damage to the Earth System?

These truths may be hard to swallow but they seem to me to be unassailable. And we do not need to know anything more to justify the new anthropocentrism because they place human beings inescapably at the center of the Earth System's evolution. Such truths mean that human agency is now more potent than ever, even if we now understand that agency not as the autonomous capacity of free beings but as a force always constrained by its embeddedness in the processes of nature.

As this suggests, modern philosophy's foundational division between the realm of necessity and the realm of freedom has broken down.[6] To understand what this reconfiguration of human agency means we must go beyond Earth System science to philosophy. At the heart of the new anthropocentrism stands the "embedded subject," a character who expresses the double truth of the human in the Anthropocene, that is, the possessor of autonomy but one always guided and constrained by its assimilation into the processes that govern the Earth System. It acknowledges that humans are agents more powerful than ever, yet confirms our ultimate inseparability from the forces of the natural world we inhabit. We emerge as a kind of tragic figure, the central agent, unable to fulfill the dream of modernity, to extricate ourselves from nature and rise above it. The new anthropocentric self does not float free like the modern subject, but is always woven into nature, *a knot in the fabric of nature*.

Embeddedness in the new view is neither local nor abstractly universal but defines an agency that is planetary, immersed in an Earth-world built by us out of nature but constrained by it, enjoying autonomy and power but increasingly up against an opponent that resists our autonomy and tightens the constraints.

Our power gives us greater responsibility than we have ever had to bear. Once humans separated from other creatures and began deliberately to use their world-making powers to modify their environments they assumed responsibility for natural systems and other animals. But now, in the Anthropocene, the fate of the Earth has become entwined with the fate of humans and our responsibility is of a new kind, risen to another level. Before our own welfare, our virtues, and our duties to one another, our inescapable responsibility for the Earth defines us as moral beings. And so, against all ethics from Kant onwards, morality is not to be found in the realm of freedom but is rooted in the realm of necessity because our duty to care for the Earth must precede all others. It belongs to us alone. We look across the unbridgeable gulf that separates us from all other beings; it is the gulf of responsibility. We have it; they don't.

The agency we speak of is a collective one, the more so as individuals report a declining sense of control over their lives and rising vulnerability in a globalized world. The power of humans inheres in institutions, systems, and cultures, so we can have the paradox of a widespread feeling of loss of personal power at the same time as the growth of human agency. Responsibility lies with those in a position to change the institutions, even if those at their helms are the prisoners of them, so that change must come from the "powerless."

It is this amplified responsibility for the Earth that is at the heart of the new anthropocentrism. While it is human-centered, it is the reverse of the stance of exploitation and control entrenched in previous anthropocentrisms. Rather than shunning or deflating human agency by embedding it in something much larger than we are, the obligation now is to embrace it, to own it. This is what I mean when I say the problem is not that we are anthropocentric but that we are not anthropocentric enough.

Comparing the new anthropocentrism with older forms, it is helpful to distinguish between normative anthropocentrism – which focuses on who has moral standing – and "teleological" anthropocentrism, which provides accounts of humankind's special place on Earth.[7] In the Bible's account, God created nature for man's use and, depending on the reading, that use may take the form of domination and exploitation or gratitude and stewardship. Hegel and Marx took the view that nature exists only in its potential and man's task is to actualize that potential by transforming, overcoming, and humanizing it.[8]

The new anthropocentrism of the Anthropocene is a kind of negative of teleological anthropocentrism. It is "teleological" because it accepts that we now infuse the whole in some way and so are joined together. Whereas the old form *declares* that humankind has a special place on Earth that gives it *moral* dominion over nature, the new form points out that humankind has *actual* power to change the course of the Earth, but draws the opposing ethical conclusion. The old form claims that the Earth provides endless bounty for the sake of humans; the new form believes that the Earth will not provide bounty unless humans take care of it. Instead of concluding that humans are free to do whatever we want on a passive Earth, the new anthropocentrism insists that on an active and fractious Earth humans are not free to do whatever we want but must restrain ourselves and restrict what we do. The old form was humanist because human destiny was thought to lie in human hands; the new is an anti-humanist anthropocentrism because the destiny of humans now lies as much in the hands of "Gaia" as in our own.

The old teleological anthropocentrism implies the normative assertion that only humans have moral standing. Like the old form, the new anthropocentrism acknowledges humans' unique moral status, but it interprets it differently. As it arises not from our rationality or by divine edict, but from the special place humans occupy as the world-making creature, rather than conferring entitlement to the Earth our power imposes a unique responsibility for it. It *elevates* human specialness in order to highlight our powers and their dangers, and so the obligations that go with them.

Most discussion of anthropocentrism today has no interest in its teleological forms but focuses on its normative implications, that is, on the question of whether things other than humans have moral standing and therefore value or rights. The new anthropocentrism is not interested in defending the singular moral standing of humans against other creatures; instead it emphasizes the unique responsibility of humans to protect the Earth and, above all, avoid dangerous disruption of the Earth System. The new anthropocentrism puts itself outside the usual debate over values, including the notion of intrinsic value. It is not a question of what does and does not have value; it is an approach to the whole. Protecting nature and, now, placating the Earth System trump all other considerations. This is the silent duty of Prometheus and applies irrespective of whether he acquired his powers by fair means (the gift of the gods) or foul (he stole them). It doesn't matter; he, and he alone, has the duty.

The duty to protect and placate the Earth System can be seen as self-justifying; it arises simply from the responsibility that goes with great power. Others may justify it in terms of its effects – for traditional anthropocentrism, the continued flourishing of humans, and, for non-anthropocentrism, the continued flourishing of other forms of life and ecosystems too. Alternatively, the duty to protect nature and placate the Earth can be justified by way of a teleological anthropocentrism such as the claim that humans were destined to be the dominant creature and this dominion always carried with it the obligation to use our special position responsibly.

It's worth responding briefly to two arguments against all anthropocentrisms. One, common to eco-philosophies of various kinds, is to mobilize ontological arguments and evidence from nature concerning our physical and spiritual dependence on our environments to assign intrinsic value to all living organisms and their ecosystems, and from there to deny any special value to humans. But with the Anthropocene upon us, those who reject the idea that humans occupy a special place, and call for the replacement of anthropocentrism with a philosophy of ecocentrism, are like the humble king who dresses in rags to wander among his people. A better sovereign he may be, but king he remains.

More recent criticism of anthropocentrism has been led by "post-humanists," a school of thought that emerged from European social critique in the 1990s. Rejection of anthropocentrism is seen as a natural extension of their critique of various forms of oppression embedded in the social order. I will elaborate on post-humanism in the next chapter, but its essential strategy has been to challenge human power over nature by stressing our complete immersion in it. Post-humanists highlight the "agency" of other creatures and natural systems (and even dead objects) and spread human agency among a multiplicity of natural agents. It is a move that repudiates our distinctiveness as world-makers at the very moment our unique world-transforming power reaches a climax. The new anthropocentrism, while agreeing that humans must be understood as participants in natural processes, does not attempt to dilute human agency but elevates it to a new level.

Turning to the second argument, both eco-philosophy and post-humanism look to pre-modern ontologies for responses to modern anthropocentrism, ontologies that blur the boundaries between humans and nature. Such a call means discarding Western science, which is not only impossible in practice but would mean ditching what is arguably humankind's greatest achievement (a claim to reflect upon when next in the dentist's chair). Moreover, surviving in the Anthropocene will depend on science, even if it depends more on politics. Just as we cannot turn back the geological clock, we cannot turn back the ontological clock.

Finally, calling for the adoption of some kind of mystical holism (à la Teilhard de Chardin) is anachronistic, partly for the reasons given above and partly because the new focus on the Earth System brings us down to earth. With its repudiation of atomism and reductionism, Teilhardian holism may seem consistent with the broad vision of the Earth System, but as philosophy it eviscerates its scientific content by attempting to levitate above it, into that ethereal layer of consciousness that Teilhard says surrounds the Earth and that he names the noösphere. Unlike the first two arguments, this kind of transcendent holism exalts humankind to a unique place, but detaches us from the actual world, and does so just at the time we realize how inescapably rooted we are in the Earth itself.

A difficulty common to alternatives to anthropocentrism is that they imagine that adopting or adapting a non-Western philosophy of nature can constitute a political answer to ecological destruction in the Anthropocene. It is true that the philosophy of nature developed in this work (better described as a human–Earth philosophy) looks upon non-Western cosmologies respectfully. It does so not to seek answers from them but only to wonder whether they may contain an *orientation* that may help lay the foundations for an after-modernity philosophy of the Anthropocene. Yet it remains thoroughly Western in the sense that it emerges directly from a world created by the West, the industrial capitalism that flourished there and colonized the world.

The world-making creature

In the last chapter I noted the strenuous resistance to the choice of the term "Anthropocene" because of its tendency to seduce us into locating the new epoch within the history of the species, instead of the specific history of European capitalism. (Or, as I prefer, the history of techno-industrialism, which includes various forms of socialism.) After observing that with the arrival of the Anthropocene human history and geological history converge, Dipesh Chakrabarty grapples with the question of how we can think the Anthropocene as a *species* question rather than one of social formations alone. Without denying the fact that the archetypal *anthropos* of anthropogenic climate change has been male, wealthy, and white, he pursues the intuition that the history of capital must be mixed somehow with the history of the species, that is, with deep history. "How do we relate to a universal history of life," he asks, " ... while retaining what is of obvious value in our postcolonial suspicion of the universal?"[9]

This striving for a new history of species thinking attracts no sympathy from historians Andreas Malm and Alf Hornborg.[10] There is nothing in the climate crisis or the Anthropocene that can be attributed to "mankind in general," they insist. They are hostile to the undifferentiated "anthropos" in the naming of the new epoch, for if we talk of the geology of mankind in general then the new epoch "must have its roots in the properties of that being." It is *divisions* between humans rather than any homogeneity that we must look to for the origins of "sociogenic" climate change. The risk of species talk, they argue, is that it will see analysis descend into "mystification and political paralysis."

What kind of mystification? Lisa Sideris has noticed the kinship of Chakrabarty's species talk with the family of "story of the universe" narratives associated with Teilhard de Chardin and, more recently, E. O. Wilson and Thomas Berry.[11] The latter's story of cosmic evolution has been turned by Brian Swimme and Mary Evelyn Tucker into a multimedia project telling the story of "a wondrous view of cosmic evolution as a process based on immense creativity, connection, and interdependence," one in which humans are "the mind and heart of the vast evolving universe." Sideris points to the affinity of this kind of cosmic thinking with the "good Anthropocene" stories of ecomodernism, ones that gloss over the actual causes and dangers of ecological destruction to focus on the marvellous ability of the human species to transcend any obstacle and continue its inexorable rise to a golden future. She suggests that Chakrabarty's attempts to meld the history of capitalism with a history of the species risks falling into the same trap, despite his own warnings.

These criticisms of Malm, Hornborg, Sideris, and others are well made and well taken. Yet staying within the traditional categories of social analysis and humanistic thinking cannot capture the monumental scale of the rupture in Earth and human history known as the Anthropocene, which calls on us to think in terms of the human condition and the place of humans on Earth, above and beyond the particular social conditions of the twentieth and early twenty-first centuries. Even at the level of political analysis, established theories of social conflict cannot explain it coherently.[12] How can we ascribe ecological destruction to the hegemonic power of capital when the broad populace, whose future is being destroyed, has collaborated so willingly in it? In the case of climate change, despite corporate attempts to manipulate opinion and undermine science, it is not generally true that corporate power has somehow thwarted public demand for deep cuts in carbon emission. A sustained and expanding activist campaign has made important gains, but has done so mostly in the face of public apathy. While national circumstances have varied widely (ecological consciousness in Germany is far ahead of that in the United States), public demand for the kind of rapid transition required by the science has been patchy and fickle. In recent decades the public has been depoliticized, losing the sense that alternative ways of social organization may be possible, and the ever-deepening penetration of consumerism has meant the public sees itself as having a stake in the very system that is jeopardizing the conditions of life. If the invention of the lies of climate deniers can be attributed to Exxon, the willingness to believe them cannot be. The seeds of doubt have been broadcast on fertile soils.

So if the specific human activities that gave us the Anthropocene are rooted in technological industrialism, the susceptibilities behind the refusal to change course are not. I have elsewhere enumerated the various psychological "coping strategies" we use to evade, deflate, and deny the discomforting facts of climate change.[13] They are not merely psychological proclivities. These forms of resistance are culturally embedded and socially organized – from the power of corporations to promote doubt, to the fetish of economic growth, to faith in the technofix, to the short-termism of political structures, and the innate self-absorption of consumerism. Even so, evasion and denial remain human qualities, as we have known at least since the time of the Book of Job.

Is there a way through the dilemma in which both the particular and the universal conceptions, taken alone, fail? We must somehow locate the rise of industrial capitalism within the broader arc of the history of the species and its disconcerting entanglement with geology. Without such a context the arrival of technological industrialism in the late eighteenth century is understood as a historical accident, born of the contingency opened up by random technological breakthroughs coupled with colonial adventurism and power shifts in England, in which case it has no link to the history of the species.

Chakrabarty himself believes we "stumbled into" the new era. But if a notion of the species is to be part of the story, then the rise of techno-industrialism must in some sense be contained within the larger history of humankind, that is, within a dynamic that belongs to humans in general rather than modern industrial ones, but which found its particular expression in techno-industrialism. Appeals to natural greed, the restless desire to assert dominance, or some genetically imprinted competitiveness are impossible to defend anthropologically. Nothing in "human nature" can plausibly lead to the Anthropocene. After all, it arrives after 193,000 years of humans doing not much at all except migrate and struggle to survive, followed by 7,000 years of agriculture and civilization, 300 years of industry, and 70 years of rampant growth that has seen us breach the planet's natural boundaries.

The first step to a resolution is to set aside the category of "species," which is inescapably biological, where *Homo sapiens* is merely the endpoint of one branch of the tree of life. When species thinking is imported uncritically into explanations of the Anthropocene then the scientistic epistemology of that kind of thinking is imported too. Talk of "species history" cannot get beyond biological history.

We must think in terms of the history of *humankind* instead of the history of the species, with the emphasis on the uniqueness of humans rather than what we share with other organisms – ecological limits, competition for resources, genetic inheritance, and so on.[14] The uniqueness of humans in general makes possible the particular historical conditions (divisions, social structures, inventions, politics) that were the Anthropocene's immediate cause.

It is our *world-making capacity* that makes humans unique. This is true even if there are always finite limits on the kinds of worlds we can make, and even if the worlds we make may contain the seeds of their own destruction. Humans only become human in worlds of social and material practices, including collective identity formation, language, understandings of nature, and relations of humans to the natural world. Everything we do and think occurs within worlds of lived experience embedded in a material environment. At the deepest level, worlds are modes of being, such as the human–nature ontologies that Philippe Descola divides into four types (naturalism, animism, totemism, and analogism, considered in the next chapter) and within which humans are situated and so understand themselves as beings.[15] We all inhabit worlds within worlds, so that within the modern (naturalist) world we may be caught up in the "world of business," the "world of science," the "world of ideas," and so on.

Contrary to the modern dream (founded in Kant) that the spontaneous capacity to make worlds is limitless, we now understand that world-making (like the subject who makes them) is always situated, always embedded, so that the worlds we make are never solely our creations, and the Modern dreams of infinite world-creation are always subject to the centripetal pull of Earth.

So worlds change. As a rule humans do not create worlds as a deliberate plan; such worlds grow up behind our backs. Our activities and ideas make new worlds and as they change we come to change our understanding of ourselves, and of nature. The complex world or worlds of modernity took a couple of centuries to become dominant in the West (and of course remnants of earlier worlds persisted), and it was this world that was exported by various forms of colonialism where it clashed, and still clashes, with other worlds.

Now a new world-in-the-making, Anthropocene world, is being disclosed to us. Earth System science initiated the disclosure. Its discovery of the Earth System and naming of the Anthropocene has shown the untenability of the old world and we begin to grope our way toward new worlds of lived experience. Earth System science asks us to think of the Earth in a new way, and incites us to think of humans afresh, first in terms of our material-technological capabilities as a planet-altering force, but inevitably in terms of our essential relationship to the planet. So Earth System science has simultaneously *disclosed* a condition that we already live in, one of massive human disruption of Earth System processes, and *discovered* a world that is only just emerging, the post-rupture world of a new kind of human, opening a horizon of meanings, modes of perception, ways of speaking, and possibilities for action. It has exposed both a hidden truth about humans and their environment and opened up a new truth about humans and the planet on which worlds are made. The exposure of the hidden truth is decentering the old world and pointing toward the construction of the new. If Earth System science is a paradigm shift in the earth sciences, then it is prompting an ontological shift in self-understanding and the human–Earth relation, although it is tragically true that the science is decades ahead of the zeitgeist.

So when (as we'll see in the next chapter) post-humanists and ontological turners attack subject–object dualism as false, they are saying that it does not ring true from outside the modern world. They place themselves (abstractly) outside of modern ontology to make the criticism, and they succeed in exposing the falsity of modernity's belief in its own "objectivity." But from within modernity (and we must all be situated somewhere) subject–object dualism has a truth. Naturalism as the Western way of being is not merely a set of beliefs; it is a way of *being* that makes beliefs possible. If it has been damaging to nature, it has also been enormously powerful in changing the conditions of life. Transcending subject–object dualism cannot be achieved by asking the Moderns to situate themselves in an animist or any other pre-modern ontology. Such an exhortation makes no sense. If the duality is to be transcended in some form – and Earth System thinking compels us to – then it will only be done by subjects struggling to operate within the Anthropocene world and being transformed into "post-subjects" in the process, even if the crisis world is not yet fully intelligible and so far lacks a new language to make it so.

The immediate explanation of the Anthropocene lies in the particular world built by the Moderns, the constellation of social, economic, and technological forces that gave rise to the world of the Industrial Revolution in Europe and its subsequent development in various forms, including the post-war Great Acceleration. This explanation points to the unequal and exploitative origins of the ecological crisis in the social order, and it is this frame through which political and policy solutions are typically assessed. From this viewpoint it is right to point out that the impacts of the Anthropocene fall more heavily on the poor, including the poor in rich countries.

This is history as generally understood. But beyond it we begin to see the Anthropocene in the context of an Earth history, a history that includes the generation of a world-making creature, the one that has now become a geological agent. How does this view of humans as world-makers justify the naming of the new epoch after humans in general, even though it was brought about by certain humans operating in a particular world, that of modernity? It does so because the Anthropocene is changing the material context in which all worlds can now be thought, and made. If human existence is always situated, now it can be situated only in the Anthropocene world. If the subject is always embedded, the world in which it is embedded is the Anthropocene world.

The emphasis on situated worldliness avoids the biologism of species talk and the mystification that surrounds universal stories of cosmic evolution, narratives in which worldless humans either grunt like beasts or float like angels. And it helps us to gain a deeper understanding of the modern worlds of techno-industrialism that have been the direct cause of the new epoch.

The new anthropocentrism versus ecomodernism

The new anthropocentrism might be misunderstood as close to ecomodernism and its all-powerful Kantian subject. In fact, it is radically different. It is true that both understand humans as occupying the central place with a unique transformative role on Earth; yet ecomodernism remains entrenched in the humanist tradition in which human "spontaneity" and creativity make the future. The new understanding is anti-humanist because it recognizes the hard constraints on world-making imposed by a finite and untameable Earth.

Whereas the ecomodernists see a "humanized Earth" as inevitable and desirable, for the new anthropocentrism a humanized Earth, expressed now as an Earth System disturbed by human activity, is neither inevitable nor desirable. In fact, the kind of humanized Earth we now live on is what we always had to fear, the one made by the misuse of our creative powers. While ecomoderns see humans as essentially benign, the new anthropocentrism sees them as highly ambivalent – capable of enormous creative renewal but equally capable of catastrophic hubris and overreach. The new anthropocentrism views the whole not as ultimately benevolent but as always suspended between good and evil, or rather between sustaining us and destroying us, with no tacit faith that it will all turn out well in the end. Indeed the capricious and uncontainable power of nature always threatens to come roaring into action should we push it too hard. As we now have. The absence of this sense of the countervailing power of nature, which must always be respected and feared, goes a long way towards explaining why ecomoderns can sugarcoat the Anthropocene with a layer of naïve hopefulness.

And so for today's ecomoderns, technologically sophisticated humans are quite capable of transcending temporary environmental setbacks, as if having tamed nature we must now take its place. They give a resounding "No," then a "Yes," to the questions of Nietzsche's madman who ran into the marketplace to ask of those who ushered in modernity by killing off God: "Is not the greatness of this deed too great for us? Must we ourselves not become gods simply to appear worthy of it?" For the ecomoderns at the Breakthrough Institute, "humans appear fully capable of continuing to support a burgeoning population by engineering and transforming the planet."[16] For them, the inborn dynamic of Progress means the negativity of ecological damage is sublated or assimilated into a positive force for change. The outcome is the product of a collaboration between a compliant but resilient nature and a creative species whose hegemony is ordained. If in theology man is the creation of God in his image, and therefore always subject to a greater power, in the ecomoderns' anthropology man is the creature of nature as its highest living form. This nature is not a power that rules over man; the tables are turned, and man rules over nature.

For the ecomoderns, the Anthropocene's manifestation as a system-crisis does not represent regress but makes possible, through its overcoming, a leap to a higher stage. It is not that the suffering of this world will be compensated by the rewards of another, but that the sufferings that may have to be endured in the short term will be vindicated in the marvelous world created in the good, the *great*, Anthropocene. We will cultivate a planetary garden, in the words of ecomodernism's chief spokesmen, where "nearly all of us will be prosperous enough to live healthy, free, and creative lives."[17] If, say the ecomoderns, critics of the system could escape their self-imposed despondency they would see that the opposition between humans and nature can be reconciled, and that climate change is a trial to be met and won with technology. Not only is it too soon to give up on Utopia, the Anthropocene is the kick in the pants we need finally to reach it.

Although the ecomoderns write as humanists, they construe the new epoch in a way that is structurally a theodicy, that is, a theological argument that aims to prove the ultimate benevolence of God. In Christian apologetics the first attempted proof of God's goodness in a world of suffering is usually attributed to Augustine,[18] and later taken up by Leibniz, who (in his book *Theodicy*) argued that evil acts, when we take a larger perspective, are necessary to the functioning of the whole. What may appear to us as monstrous crimes to which God acquiesces must be understood as in the service of his greater, if mysterious, benevolence. In Leibniz's pithy aphorism: "Everything happens for the best" or, in the troubling words of Alexander Pope, "Whatever is, is right." It was a sentiment satirized by Voltaire in the shape of Dr Pangloss, who, after being reduced to the state of syphilitic beggar, clung to his sunny outlook. His endearing personality trait became his deluded philosophy of life.

So theodicy is a response to the existence of evil in a world created by a benevolent God. It did not take long for a vigorous theological dispute to become secularized.[19] Hegel's philosophical system saw evil subsumed in the larger movement of world history, whose goal and endpoint is the full actualization of Spirit or Mind. To take this view required Hegel to cleave to the idea, common then as now, that the world moves according to some "ultimate design," in his case the unfolding of self-consciousness. However much we may recoil from its particulars, the world unfolds as it ought to – along the path to a glorious finale. In this way, evil is elevated to the metaphysical sphere and is no longer a merely moral question. After Hegel, Marx too rejected moral explanations for suffering, but he brought evil down from the metaphysical sphere to the material one; the immiserization of the proletariat became a necessary stage in the attainment of a classless Utopia.

The ecomodernist "good Anthropocene" argument is founded on a belief in the ultimate benevolence of the whole, a goodness that in the end transcends and defeats the structural obstacles, sufferings, and moral lapses that seem to threaten it. That this belief is rarely voiced only bespeaks its secret power. In the world of the good Anthropocene the new geological epoch is greeted not as imminent peril but as a "forward-looking vision of the planet" or, in the words of *An Ecomodernist Manifesto*, as "an optimistic view toward human capacities and the future"; indeed they see the coming of a *great* Anthropocene, one of "universal human dignity on a biodiverse and thriving planet."[20]

Climate change is viewed as a treatable side-effect of the modernization process, a growing pain that the growth process itself will resolve. Whereas in Leibniz's theodicy God's will ensures all is for the good, for the ecomoderns it is Progress driven by human creativity and urge to betterment that ensures good will prevail. So in place of a *theo*dicy they instate an "*anthropo*dicy" in which human-directed Progress takes the place of God. The goodness that will prevail does not reside in the hearts of men and women but in the order of things, an order that mobilizes the creativity and resourcefulness of humans. In the end the ecomoderns' commitment to the good Anthropocene is a secular manifestation of the idea of Providence, with Man rather than God guiding human destiny. We have seen the future, and it is good.

The structure of the "good Anthropocene" argument is essentially a Hegelian theodicy; evil, here read as ecological damage, is construed as a contradiction essential to driving history forward toward the realization of the Absolute, here read as unstoppable progress toward universal prosperity. Hegel inscribed his theodicy into the process of the unfolding of human freedom, which will "enable us to comprehend all the ills of the world, including the existence of evil, so that the thinking spirit may be reconciled with the negative aspects of existence."[21]

In the eighteenth and nineteenth centuries theodicy attracted fierce controversy. Immanuel Kant attacked it as immoral and blasphemous because it goes beyond what we can know about God. If we cannot know what God wants "we cannot judge what is best for the whole."[22] A Kantian argument against the good Anthropocene might be that we cannot know the ultimate outcome of the Anthropocene because it is beyond our capacity to predict the Earth System's behavior and beyond our capacity to control it, the more so after the recent rupture to its functioning. The Earth always retains something mysterious and inaccessible – an "indivisible remainder" – and in the transition from the Holocene to the Anthropocene new forces have been unleashed that we can only ever understand imperfectly, and regulate even less.

Yet it is not only the "mysterious" unwillingness of the Earth System to subject itself to human regulation that upends the ecomodernist position, but also their curious unwillingness to acknowledge the manifest failure of humans to create social structures and institutions consistent with the sustained flourishing of the biosphere we inhabit, and their determination to continue making worlds that are incompatible with the possibilities provided by the Earth.

The theodicy-like structure of the good Anthropocene argument also alerts us to its essential political and moral flaw. Theodicy was condemned by its critics because it led to *quietism*; if suffering is justified because it serves God's larger purpose we must accept it calmly and not attempt to change the world. We should leave it to Providence, human destiny under God's guidance, a "grandiose calculation," writes Paul Ricoeur, that is wrecked by "the complaint of the righteous sufferer."[23] Ecomodernists are not quietists who sit in contemplation awaiting the good Anthropocene's arrival; instead, they want to smooth its path. Their political engagement is directed toward facilitating the attainment of that which is ordained, which in practice involves an inordinate emphasis on nuclear energy. Their task is to protect and defend the system so that it has the chance to fulfill its promise.

In her study of theodicy, *Evil in Modern Thought*, Susan Neiman observed that "Providence is a tool invented by the rich to lull those whom they oppress into silent endurance."[24] The same may be said for the invention of the good Anthropocene: for the victims inclined to protest against the system, the golden promise of a new dawn lulls them into silent endurance. To the sufferers it says: "Do not blame the system, for you it is the only source of hope."

(In praise of technology)

While early discussion of the Anthropocene has focused on human disruption of the planet's ecosystems, the deeper significance of the new epoch is the evidence of the unpredictable, fractious, and unfathomable responses of the planet to human influence on its processes. If the Earth is "fighting back," techno-utopian responses – like solar geoengineering aimed at controlling the global climate system through regulating the amount of sunlight reaching the planet – may be seen as a last-ditch attempt by eco-modernists to impose order, to exercise mastery, to regulate the planet as a whole in the interests of humans. For as long as we entertain hopes of technologies of planetary control we can avoid facing the disturbing questions that the climate crisis thrusts upon us. For some, the idea of regulating the amount of solar radiation falling on the planet is hubris on steroids; for others, it has a tranquilizing effect. The natural world is pacified and our capacity to manipulate and turn it to our own ends is reaffirmed. While Earth System science challenges the conception of humans as lords of the Earth, techno-utopianism and strong interpretations of consequentialist philosophy fortify our sense of domination over it. Instead of being jolted by the harsh warnings of climate scientists and the early manifestations of a transformed climate, this affirmation leaves us floating in a warm bath of self-belief and contented hopes for the future. Terry Eagleton's observation is germane: "Optimists are conservatives because their faith in a benign future is rooted in their trust in the essential soundness of the present."[25]

It might be thought that the criticisms ventured above reflect an absence of faith in human inventiveness and the munificence of technology. In fact, my argument is not anti-technological but the reverse. Creativity – including, but by no means confined to, its expression as technological invention – is the defining quality of human beings, the world-making creatures. Our task on Earth is to use that creativity to transform the world around us in ways that allow humans *and* the natural world to flourish and strive to reach their boundless potential. While technology holds the greatest promise to attain this end, it also harbors the greatest danger; or, since the reification of technology is at the heart of the problem, it is more accurate to say that technology embedded in certain social structures and institutions represents the greatest danger.

The risk has always been that a respectful appreciation of our inventive powers would take the form of a megalomania in which humans mimic the God of Genesis by aspiring to a "second creation" on Earth. A second creation was first imagined in Francis Bacon's seventeenth-century vision of a technological Utopia overseen by the College of the Six Days Work. Fredrik Albritton Jonsson traces the vision's practical manifestations in improvements in English agriculture and the conception of engineered landscapes.[26] But it also spawned an anthropo-supremacism expressed, for example, in the ideology of manifest destiny that warranted and energized the nineteenth-century conquest of the American west by settlers who took technology to be a gift of God that would help them transform the New World into a Garden of Eden. The vision of a second creation reached its secular zenith in the post-war decades of the twentieth century in the United States, sparked perhaps by the undreamed-of power of nuclear fission. Its rootedness in the American psyche helps to explain why faith in climate engineering is stronger in the United States than in Europe and why the precautionary principle holds less appeal there (and perhaps too why some evangelical Christians have boarded cruise ships to the melting Antarctic where they have been caught broadcasting seeds in the expectation that the newly exposed continent will blossom into a new Eden).[27]

After Bacon, warnings soon flowed from the pens of witnesses like Wordsworth, Hölderlin, and John Ruskin concerning the perils of aspiring to omnipotence.[28] Later critics – from Spengler to Heidegger to George Orwell – believed the craving for control over nature would inevitably spill into the desire to control humans. What is remarkable, however, is not so much that technology has come to dominate humans but that humans have so willingly subjugated themselves to it. How cheaply we have surrendered our autonomy.

For Bacon, science and technology exerted their influence on a neutral and passive Earth, and the possibility of its spoliation did not occur to his council of wise men. Yet the reality was apparent to some by the end of the eighteenth century when the ugly stains of industry on countryside and town began to attract resistance. The misgivings expressed by Romantics such as Hölderlin and Novalis were widespread. Goethe took a more nuanced stance. For him, as an expression of human creativity, industrialization was to be embraced. Yet, as Adrian Wilding tells us, in *Faust II* he recognized both the enormous attractions of human technological feats as well as their moral dangers.[29] For Goethe, human creativity is a divine gift, one that tests our character. Would we use it to separate ourselves from God and usurp His power, or would we apply it with the humility that goes with such a blessing? For Faust, beyond all the fleeting pleasures of the flesh he meets, only the temptation to use our God-like power to create a Utopia through mechanical means – "Till earth is reconciled to man" – can bring him to the point of losing his wager and surrendering his soul. The divine gift of technological power came with a condition – we must use it in a morally responsible way, otherwise it will come to rule us.

In the spirit of Goethe, my argument is not anti-technological; it celebrates human creativity but warns against the tendency to hubris. Technology brings gifts that inspire our daily gratitude and yet the "technocratic paradigm," in Pope Francis's phrase, also threatens to be our downfall, and no more so than in the recourse to geoengineering schemes such as spraying sulphate particles into the upper atmosphere to regulate the total amount of sunlight reaching the planet. Equally, technology is the means through which humankind may release the full bounty of the gift of nature, and therefore represents the opportunity to respect that gift, while conscious of the ever-present danger of its domination over economic and political life.

3 Friends and Adversaries

Grand narratives are dead, until now

Grand narratives that order and explain human experience are out of fashion. Reading laws into the unfolding human record seems to deprive humans of their autonomy and diversity. Powered by the force of universal reason, the grand narratives of the past – from the progressive victory of Reason over superstition, modernization theory and the inexorable spread of liberal capitalism to the dialectical flowering of Spirit and all Utopias on Earth – buried worlds of difference beneath a Eurocentric ideology. Their explicit or implicit teleology of universal human progress could not be defended after the privileged place of the male European understanding of the world had been exposed. The enlightened view today is that humans make their own futures in a thousand diverse if culturally conditioned ways, and there is no direction to our collective existence on Earth.

Beyond its inherent chauvinism, faith in the grand narrative of modernity came up against disappointment over its broken promises. Progress as history's motor began to be seen as a myth serving the interests of the powerful, one that kept the powerless immobilized with imaginary pots of gold at the end of history's rainbow. The metanarrative was, in Lyotard's phrase, an "apparatus of legitimation" rendered increasingly obsolescent by the incredulity of the (excluded,) and indeed every one of us who lives at the intersection of several narratives. ✘ unlucky

Yet the failure of modernity's story of a universal humanity joined in a common project does not mean there can never be a story that draws all humans together. Does not the arrival of the Anthropocene justify new grounds for an emerging narrative of humanity as a whole? The Anthropocene arrives as the totalizing event par excellence. Local worlds still matter, of course; but Earth System science tells us that we live on the Earth, which is not merely a collection of many local worlds but a dynamic, evolving total entity above and beyond the local, and increasingly deciding the fate of all locals.

If not every human is responsible for bringing on the Anthropocene, every human is destined to live in it. A new narrative of narratives cannot be a simple reinvention of the old, for the first lesson of the Anthropocene is that a new "philosophy of history" must be a merged history of humans and Earth taken together. In this sense a new grand narrative is not one imposed from above through the synthesizing of historical trends; it is forced on us from below by the convergence of human and geological history.

If the repudiation of the power of universal reason to explain the progress of history carries with it the rejection of grand narratives, then what might be the new story emerging in the Anthropocene? It is the narrative of the human ventured in this book, of life lived and ordered under the shadow of the new geological epoch, in which the local is increasingly dominated by the global, where the events of history are already showing the stamp of global environmental change, where lives are more and more sensitive to "natural" events with a human finger-print, and where relations between states increasingly center on managing and adapting to a recalcitrant Earth. It is a narrative whose force increasingly draws together diverse events under the umbrella of a "humanized nature," the key to which is found not so much in local practices and understandings but in the implacable logic of Earth System science. It is a human–nature narrative that demands a reorientation of cultural production, of aesthetic creativity drawn to the vast transformation the new epoch brings.

While it collects together all humans in its story, it diverges from all previous metanarratives in what it promises, or, rather, in what it does not promise. It does not promise universal freedom or the flowering of human potential, but the reverse. There is no promise of a happy ending in the Anthropocene narrative. It is not a story we *want* to believe in; it is one we are compelled to accept. The new narrative brought by the Anthropocene invites us to open ourselves to a shift in the zeitgeist, from the late Holocene's cheer-ful promise of prosperity to the brooding defensiveness of the early Anthropocene.

It is true that compared with older ones such a narrative comes into the world with a handicap. How can it mobilize a social movement if it is born of failure and cannot promise pro-gress? Yet it is enough for a narrative to serve a truth-telling func-tion, to explain where we are and who we are becoming. After all the old narratives promised progress but failed to tell us the truth, serving as rationalizations for what those in their spell wanted to do anyway. If I am arguing in support of a narrative of fiasco, of being too late, then its truth holds out the promise that the worst can still be avoided.

If the grand narratives of modernity lent legitimacy to the prevailing order and structure of power relations, the arrival of the Anthropocene serves to delegitimize their claims. If, as post-modern critics suggest, science is a legitimizing narrative for the prevailing order, then the prevailing order now finds itself under siege from science. The new narrative does not serve the powerful but exposes their absolute failure.

Yet, like the narrative of the Moderns, the coming Anthropocene narrative *does* appeal to a kind of universal reason – the logic of Earth System science that has been painstakingly put together over the last three or four decades and continues to evolve. No appeal to cultural perspectives can get around the blunt truth of the Earth System, this awkward object that has moved into our vision and is set to stay. If the postmodern moves in a world of knowledge, language, and text, the Anthropocene brings us back to Earth with a thud. But it can be of no comfort to the Moderns' faith in the power of universal reason as the guide to action, for it betrays the presumption that the inner spirit of reason is benign, that its application inevitably serves the good.

So we have been drawn into the orbit of the Earth System, and can no longer believe we inhabit only our local and regional environments. Earth System science has given us a story about the Earth as a whole. It is one in which humans, and not wealthy white people alone, have entered into deep history to become a force of nature whose influence is to be inscribed in the Geological Time Scale.

Recognition of this epochal truth came to some at the climate change conference held in Paris late in 2015. The antagonism between North and South that had plagued the previous 20 conferences was no longer the dominant mood of the negotiations. The larger countries of the South – with the exception of India – had realized that it was no longer enough for them simply to demand that the North fix the problem it had created; they too were becoming responsible for warming. And the threat to their populations had become more real as the scientific warnings sank in. The North's failure to fix the problem it had created was, and remains, unforgivable; yet the narrative in which the South points the finger of blame at the North had shifted to one in which "humankind must act," because the situation had changed. Years of campaigning by citizens' groups in North and South were finally bearing fruit.

Before the 2009 conference in Copenhagen, China's Premier Wen Jiabao was emphasizing the West's historical obligations, and China then sabotaged the negotiations.[1] Six years later such a stance was no longer possible. Remember, China is now the world's biggest carbon-emitting country by a long way, and the average Chinese person is responsible for more greenhouse gas emissions than the average European. Emissions from the South will soon exceed those of the North and it is likely that in a couple of decades the total historical emissions of the South will exceed those of the North. To the extent that climate change is the primary cause of human disturbance of the functioning of the Earth System, these facts mean that responsibility for bringing on the Anthropocene is increasingly shared between North and South.

Although the experience of the Anthropocene as it unfolds will vary widely, with the world's poor and vulnerable the most undeserving victims, the wealthy will not escape. Or not for long. The power elites who gather annually in Davos will not be exempted from the effects of mass population movements, political turmoil, and geopolitical conflict. The world's central banks are anxious about the possibility of a global financial crisis in response to sudden write-downs in the asset value of energy corporations. Moreover, the daily lives of the rich and the middle classes are wholly dependent on centralized infrastructures to deliver energy, water, and food into their homes. If those systems break down they will be helpless. And it is a well-grounded fact that as people become wealthier they also become more distressed when they must give up some of their privilege. Change will extract a high psychological cost.

And so in Paris the leaders of all countries gathered to attempt to agree on a collective solution to a common threat. It is true that some nations insisted on more far-reaching commitments – with the small island states holding a special moral claim – while others spoke grandly in public and practiced obstructionism in private. Yet the fact is that presidents and prime ministers from virtually every nation assembled for the purpose of acting cooperatively under a united will to protect their homelands from the common threat of global warming, and to undertake the seemingly impossible task of negotiating a settlement allocating a fair contribution of each state to the shared task. Nowhere in the history of diplomacy have all 195 nations come together in this way, each having first presented to the rest of world their 10-, 20-, or 30-year national plans to transform their energy economies. It is a hard truth that those plans taken together still fall well short of attaining the common goal, yet the question the nations of the world sought to answer was clear: how can we all live together on this Earth? At the end of the eighteenth century Immanuel Kant foresaw a historical process of growing cosmopolitanism among free and rational peoples, yet it is the forces of nature, rather than the attraction of global citizenship, driving humans together.

In a postmodern age that celebrates diversity and pluralism, a second force in addition to the Anthropocene has arrived to unite humankind in a way that lends itself to a new narrative of narratives. The entire world has fallen under the spell of the hydra-headed monster known as globalization. Its leading objective has been to dismantle economic borders – for finance capital, tax liabilities, trade, intellectual property, and, increasingly, skilled labor. Above this material homogenization, the spread of the culture of the market is almost complete. For popular culture, think Disney, Facebook, Zara, McDonald's, Apple, Longines, James Bond, Mr Bean, and *The X Factor*; they shape consciousness and desire in the favelas, kampongs, and shantytowns as much as they do in the suburbs. The astonishing force of consumer culture has swamped traditional customs, values, and aspirations, replacing them with a devotion to money, materialism, and branded identities that has left tradition a smoking rubble. Even jihadists bent on destroying the West expertly use social media to build their brand. Although lamented by older novelists, artists, and cultural observers, this force is unstoppable and now provides the barely noticed wallpaper of daily life, especially for the young.

It should be said that if everyone is drawn into a global system of production, consumption, and culture this is not to say that those so drawn are becoming citizens of the world, members of the "universal brotherhood" of Schiller's "Ode to Joy," a force to "re-unite what custom's sword has divided." Arguably, the more we become self-focused global consumers, the less we are oriented toward global citizenship.

Hegel once wrote that, in the development of freedom, world history travels from East to West – "for Europe is the absolute end of history, just as Asia is the beginning."[2] Today world history has made the return journey, now loaded up with the baggage of Western ideology, the heaviest piece of which I have labeled "Growth Fetishism."[3] The era of colonialism may have ended, yet its enduring legacy has been the insatiable desire to import consumer capitalism, symbolized by the shopping mall, the Trojan horse of soft power. While the postmodern left valiantly attempts to defend cultural and social difference, and to use this difference as a way of critiquing universalizing narratives, the procession of Western values and aspirations marches on blithely across the East or, as we now prefer, the South. Difference, of course, still counts, but difference clings on under the growing hegemony of the global.

The centers of power too are making the return journey from West to East. China's sustained growth rate of 8–10 percent or more in the 1990s and 2000s – along with the West's dependence on it for trade and loans – is transferring the fate of the world to the hands of the ruling elite in Beijing, a task it may in a couple of decades share with its counterpart in New Delhi. After pursuing for two centuries a program of economic growth at all costs through rampant exploitation of the natural world, the West now hopes desperately that the East can "decouple" its economic growth from environmental destruction.

Of course, the two great totalizing forces of globalization and the Anthropocene are not unconnected. The Great Acceleration began at the end of World War II and inaugurated both phenomena. The rapid acceleration of economic growth, along with booming consumption and its profligate resource usage and waste, drove human destabilization of the Earth System. The pursuit of the American Dream at the same time brought the Anthropocene nightmare.

If the vision of mankind in general was an illusion of nineteenth-century Europe there is no reason to believe it must always remain a fantasy. If Enlightenment imaginings of liberal cosmopolitanism, with their principles of individual rights and universal truth, were accused of imperialism and absolutism,[4] one cannot accuse the judgments of Earth System science of either. And while the globalization project has been guilty of imperialism and absolutism in spades, the enthusiasm of its "victims," once drawn in, to live under its imperial rule robs the criticism of its sting.[5] And so we gaze into a future of the progressive elimination of difference in a globalized world, coupled with the dawning of an Anthropocene that, over the next decades, must increasingly rule over everyday life and consciousness wherever one resides, opening up space for a world narrative and perhaps a philosophy of global history. Above all of the diversity stand one global economy, one global culture, one total Earth.

The Anthropocene arrives as the grand narrative to progressively order and explain experience, the universal truth all humanity is obliged to live under, a narrative that, like it or not, subsumes all others and against which they will be judged. As it gathers pace the tyranny of the Earth System will overrule the plurality of local stories and cultures. If the Anthropocene performs this unexpected and unwelcome unification of humankind then it invites us to formulate a story of humankind, a narrative explanation of the progress of human history as a whole, a task I begin in the next chapter.

If this argument for an emerging world narrative of the Anthropocene stands in sharp contrast to the entire thrust of the social sciences and humanities over the last 50 years, let me now consider explicitly the intellectual trends that the new epoch challenges. By way of an organizing framework it will help to recall one of the essential truths of the science of the Anthropocene. The new epoch reflects *both* a multiplication of human power *and* an activation of dormant forces in the Earth System. Power on Earth is not a zero-sum phenomenon; the power of both humans and nature has gained strength. The new anthropocentrism put forward in this book is an attempt to accommodate this double expansion of power. Other responses to the Anthropocene can be understood more clearly when we realize that they recognize one form of power-surge but not the other, as illustrated in the table on the next page.

The following sections explore the right-hand column of the table, the contrast between the new or embedded anthropocentrism I have proposed and the post-humanism and ontological

		The Earth	
		Unchanged power	**More power**
Humans	**Unchanged** *or* **less power**	Denial	Post-humanism Ontological pluralism
	More power	Ecomodernism The system	New anthropocentrism

pluralism that dominates environmental thought. The latter have the great virtue of breaking down the Moderns' conception of a passive nature available for human domination. And the post-humanist approach has posed the vital question: how can we rethink the human after modernity? (Latour names this human the "earth-bound.") However, in assigning more power to the Earth – or more agency to nature – the post-humanists mistakenly take it away from humans. I hope to persuade them that the arrival of the Anthropocene radically changes our conception of the human and our extraordinary power in nature.

The bottom row of the table highlights the essential difference between the new anthropocentrism and ecomodernism (and the market capitalism it speaks for). Ecomodernism's self-assigned label is apt because, by failing to recognize that the Earth has been roused from its peaceful Holocene slumber and is now set on a violent and uncontrollable course, ecomodernism can continue to pursue modernism's dream of using technology to bend nature to the will of humans. If ecomodernism and the new anthropocentrism both see the human as the special creature with indisputable power on Earth, the latter does not share ecomodernism's human-istic faith that the special creature can decide its own fate. The eco-moderns are like Lilliputians who have returned to town satisfied they have shackled the giant, oblivious to the fact that Gulliver has stirred, snapped his puny bonds, and (unlike in Swift's fable) is seriously pissed off.

After post-humanism

For half a century, the trend in the social sciences and human-ities has been to deconstruct all social hierarchies of power and control. Feminism set out to cut men down to size; queer theory destabilized heteronormativity; and postcolonial and subaltern studies wrote "history from below" to delegitimize the stories from above. They worked by holding humanism to account, by turning its principles of equality, human dignity, and justice against the societies that proclaimed them. Yet, as if reaching the end of their long march through the catalogue of discrimination and oppres-sion, from the early 1990s some critical social scientists turned their attention to a new target – human domination of nature, criticism of which had previously been confined to a handful of ecologists and eco-philosophers (albeit with wide influence outside the academy). Beyond Eurocentrism, androcentrism and heteronormativity, the new focus became anthropocentrism itself. Although it felt like the continuation of radical social criticism, in fact the shift from critique within the human world to critique of the human world's relation to nature was an unwarranted episte-mological leap that drains the approach of its legitimacy.

This "post-humanism" has swept through the social sciences, drawing together postcolonial studies, post-natural anthropology, feminist theory, eco-philosophy, and science and technology studies, in a common deconstruction of modernity's narrative of human domination of the Earth. It begins from the verdict that the original crime of modernity was the "Cartesian" division between subject and object and so the radical separation of humans from nature. Jason Moore puts it explicitly: "Just as we have been learning to move beyond the dualisms of race, gender, sexuality, and Eurocentrism over the past four decades, it is now time to deal with the source of them all: the Nature/Society binary."[6] Although the causal links are left vague, to this division are attributed all the ills and crimes of the West, and especially the wanton destruction of nature. The dualistic European ontology is said to form the philosophical basis for anthropocentrism and for claims of the superiority of societies that have become "enlightened" through science and reason, that is, by breaking the spell of the enchantment of the natural world. Post-humanist intellectuals share, in Alf Hornborg's words, "the conviction that the Enlightenment view of nature is inextricably tied to colonial European ambitions to dominate the world."[7] By implication, the horrors of colonial conquest were legitimized by the new view of nature.

The post-humanist understanding is today the most influential critique of the prevailing order – the system of technological industrialism and profit-driven consumerism that gave rise to the ecological crisis. By turning its attention to the human–nature relationship, post-humanism has deepened our understanding of the natural world, freeing it from the pure objectification imposed by the scientific revolution and industrialism, and the philosophies that grew from them. In doing so, it has destabilized the Moderns' idea of the human. Yet the rupture of the Anthropocene has created a new dispensation that exposes the weakness of the post-humanist understanding, rendering it an obstacle to grasping the situation. And so it is essential to engage with and pass beyond post-humanism. While it is constructed on an indispensable truth, a critique of the hard Cartesian division between subject and object and the separation of humans from nature, it took the critique to a place impossible to defend after the Anthropocene.

Inspired by ecological science, post-humanism insists that, for all of the Moderns' sophisticated theories of the subject and ambitions for mastery, human beings remain embedded, entangled, affiliated, and networked into the natural world. The transmogrification of humans into a force of nature, one that has disrupted the functioning of the Earth System, is the most striking confirmation imaginable of this feature of life on Earth. The Anthropocene does indeed render inescapable the fact of our deep connections with natural processes, yet it is also the most striking proof that humans do occupy a position separate from nature and from there now stand against it. Contrary to the post-humanist stance, accepting the science of the Anthropocene entails accepting the unique and extraordinary power of humans to influence, by conscious decision or otherwise, the future course of the Earth, even if it is not necessarily in the way intended.

Despite this indubitable fact, the idea of the Anthropocene has been embraced by large numbers of post-humanists in a way that *deflates* the significance and power of humans on the planet. They are drawn to the idea of the Anthropocene because it points to the ultimate failure of the modernist project of domination and because it highlights their claim that human separation from nature has always been a delusion. Yet if humans now rival the great forces of nature in our impact on the functioning of the Earth System then this fact *elevates* humans to a previously unimagined level of power over nature, and our capacity to choose to exercise this power or not marks us out as *the* unique creature.

If the new concept has been taken up with alacrity by the "non-anthropocentric humanities," determined to go beyond all humanisms, they nevertheless embrace the values of humanism – tolerance of difference, dignity of the person, and justice for all.[8] Indeed, they are today's most vigorous defenders of humanist values, directing their ire only at the narrow chauvinism within which they have traditionally been applied, first to men and whites and heterosexuals, and later to all humans to the exclusion of the rest of nature. By extending these values to other species and non-human nature the post-humanists aim to put humans in their proper place.

Here we recall the distinction I have made between, on the one hand, anthropocentrism as a description of the uniqueness of humans as a species and our actual power on Earth, and, on the other, the attitude of arrogance and mastery over nature that typically, though not necessarily, has gone with it. In order to avoid the fact of actual human domination of nature, post-humanists define anthropocentrism as a phenomenon of the human mind, "the *attitude* that presents the human species as the centre of the world, enjoying hegemony over other beings and functioning as masters of a nature which exists to serve its needs."[9] The strategy is to challenge human chauvinism by proving the hollowness of all claims to human uniqueness and our actual power over nature.

The denial of power is done by way of ontologies that, more or less extensively, *take agency away* from humans and distribute it throughout the natural world. And so at the very historical juncture at which human agency has never been more evident and pre-eminent, prominent post-humanists make claims such as: "human nature is in no way separate from nature as a whole [and] there are no fixed and necessary boundaries between the human and the animal."[10] Jane Bennett's book *Vibrant Matter* is a notable example of this "new materialist" trend, building on Latour's notion of actants, agents that may be human or non-human, alive or dead. She sets out to distribute human agency around nature, dissolving human intentionality in a soup of natural forces and objects. And so "an actant never really acts alone. Its efficacy or agency always depends on the collaboration, cooperation, or interactive interference of many bodies and forces."[11] Humans are deprived of their uniqueness.

In an early attempt to dissolve boundaries between human and non-human the influential post-humanist feminist Donna Haraway turned to primatology. For her, "human" and "nature" are cultural categories and can be made to converge, and she shows how the study of primates can pull humans into the animal world.[12] (The primatologists themselves do not make this kind of claim.) With phrases such as "refusal of binary dualisms," "a bestiary of agencies," and "natureculture" instead of nature and culture, Haraway aims to "get in the way of man making himself the Greatest Story Ever Told."[13]

Yet the blunt truth of the Anthropocene is that, in the book of life, man *is* the greatest story ever told. Or rather, to avoid ambiguity, humankind is the greatest story ever told, where "greatest" is understood to mean the most remarkable. To believe otherwise one has to convince oneself that anthropocentrism is in fact nothing more than androcentrism – and a colonialism, a rapacious capitalism, and a nature-destroying monster. Yet it is always a mistake to assume that what was had to be, the more so when in history there were countervailing forces, including post-humanism itself. Haraway declares herself a Darwinian, yet insists on snapping off the last twig of the longest branch of the tree of life, on which perches *Homo sapiens*, a twig that represents a giant leap from even our closest evolutionary relatives. To know this one needs only to turn on one's computer, connect to Wi-Fi, open YouTube, and watch Valentina Lisitsa playing Liszt's *Hungarian Rhapsody No. 2*.

Haraway's terminological incontinence – for her the Anthropocene might just as well be the "Capitalocene," the "Plantationocene," or the "Chthulucene" (*sic*) – aims at contextualizing, relativizing, and, ultimately, disempowering the conclusions of scientists,[14] although she still relies on their work for support and inspiration. This careless (one might even say arrogant!) approach to Earth System science is a baleful hangover from the social constructionist critiques of Big Science of the 1960s and 1970s and of postmodern "critique" in the 1980s (which perversely lives on most powerfully in the campaign of climate science denial).[15] The invention willy-nilly of substitute terms for the Anthropocene is itself an epistemological mistake because it treats scientific analysis as if it were the same as social analysis. When Jan Zalasiewicz commented that Paul Crutzen came up with the term at the right time, Kieran Suckling asked, "Why was the time right? Is there something about Western psychology and history that made this time right?" as if the development of a body of scientific evidence were nothing more than an emanation of social and psychological conditions.[16] If the Anthropocene is another example of Western linguistic imperialism, changing the name will not exempt the poor and vulnerable of the South from its devastating effects.

Anna Tsing, a disciple of Haraway, is also determined to cut humans down to size, arguing that the belief in human exceptionalism "blinds us" to our interdependence with other species. Anxious about the misuse of the concept of human nature made by social conservatives and sociobiologists, Tsing proposes a "human nature" in constant historical flux, depending not so much on intra-human social change but on our relationships with other species, going so far as to propose that "Human nature is an interspecies relationship."[17] We are not merely influenced by our relationships with other creatures; we are *defined* by them, and therefore embedded in a world of creatures above which it is impossible for us to rise. It is a world in which there can be no "exceptions." And no mastery, for the agency that gives rise to changes in human history is spread across the multitude of other species that define us. So, for example, humans did not domesticate cereals; "cereals domesticated humans." To counter blinkered understandings of history as an intra-human affair, Tsing develops a theory of plant and animal determination of human social structures covering social class, the state, colonialism, patriarchy, family structure, and racism. And if we want to uncover the inner meaning of the whole box and dice, then we can do no better than consult the matsutake mushroom, as she has done in *The Mushroom at the End of the World*.

Softening Tsing's absolutism, post-humanist sympathizer Tim Morton explains:

> It's not the case that we promoters of the nonhuman are trying to extinguish the human altogether, or burst outside it. We are simply allowing nonhumans to be what they are, namely entangled with us in all kinds of strange ways, neither absolutely reducible to human access nor completely divorced from it. And nonhumans get to access us, and one another.[18]

Even so, the post-humanist, or new materialist, redistribution of agency both *deflates* human power and control in the world by embedding us in material networks, and *inflates* the agency of non-human matter (dead and alive) by attributing to it the ability, through that same embedding, to control humans. The new materialists do this by sleight of hand, by the deployment of metaphors to attribute qualities to material things as if they applied literally. So, in one of the more systematic expositions of the new materialism, Timothy James LeCain writes of the non-human material world as "creating," "constituting," "shaping," "making," "producing," and "enslaving" humans; in short, "things have power over us" so that we are "in the earth's hands." Coal and oil "demand that humans conform to their material needs"; coal "helped create modern democracy" and "some very powerful material things ... have increasingly come to dictate our collective fate."[19]

A material object that produces, demands, enslaves, and dictates is one to which intention is attributed, where in fact it only has influence. The ascription of intention, and therefore choice, to dead objects or non-human animals that lack the capacity, physical and intellectual, to make and execute plans to change humans is in fact a program of *anthropomorphism* and therefore anthropocentrism by stealth. The post-humanist habit of anthropomorphizing is quite unlike that of Earth System scientists who reach for phrases like "the angry beast" to describe the Earth in the Anthropocene, knowing the reader will understand them as metaphors.

If embedded humans do indeed co-evolve with a material world, each influencing the other, it only means that humans are constrained – and empowered – to exercise their enormous power within material networks, networks that now constellate around the *anthropos* so that we are justified in naming the new epoch the Anthropocene. Moreover, if humans and the material world co-evolve, the implication that they do so in some kind of harmonious unity has to be challenged. The Anthropocene's fracture between human and Earth ruptures all harmony.

Buried in the new materialist deflation of human agency lies a quietist political philosophy. If "some very powerful material things ... have increasingly come to dictate our collective fate" we have no choices and must accept the dictatorship of things. LeCain himself takes Nietzsche's misanthropic position, suggesting that we may now be discovering that the Earth is "deeply inhospitable to intelligent hominid life." The only savior might be for us to return to a "far more ancient understanding of the material environment." Turning back the historical clock could not work in the post-Enlightenment Holocene, let alone the Anthropocene.

The story of humans-as-just-another-species cannot withstand the arrival of the Anthropocene. The new epoch is the ultimate demonstration that, however networked into the natural world we are (as the post-humanists have shown), humans do stand out.

Jason Moore attempts an awkward blend of the feminist post-humanism of Haraway and Tsing and a kind of Marxism, despite the radically humanist roots of the latter.[20] Beginning from an epistemological position that blurs the distinction between scientific facts and social facts, his argument is that the Anthropocene ought not to be defined by actual physical impacts in the world but by the deeper historical causes of those impacts, namely "relations of capital and power." He concedes that "the facts in the debate may be more-or-less correct," but dismisses as "weak" the arguments of those in the best position to know, the experts on the Anthropocene Working Group. The problem with the scientists, he tells us, is that they want to define the new geological epoch "empirically": "The Anthropocene argument takes biogeological questions and facts – turning on the presence of variously significant stratigraphic signals – as an adequate basis for historical periodization."[21]

That Moore cannot distinguish between geological history and human history is symptomatic of much contemporary critical social science. He takes to its extreme the argument that we must dissolve all Cartesian dualisms, that is, the divide between nature and culture, pursuing an ontological flat-land of entanglement. "Human activity not only produces biospheric change, but relations between humans are themselves produced by nature." And so a proper analysis of the Anthropocene would *begin* with actually existing human relationships and then "move towards geological and biophysical change." Transcending science altogether, Moore ends up rejecting the claim that we are living in the Anthropocene because it is "a curiously Eurocentric vista of humanity."[22] And the determination to reject all dualisms sees him challenge the foundational scientific claim that "humans are overwhelming the great forces of nature." We cannot overwhelm nature when we are indistinguishable from it.

How could social science come to this? The impossible contradiction in Moore's position now becomes clear. On the one hand, he wants to deny humans their power and special place with a "post-humanist" embedding of humans in nature; on the other hand, he wants to define the new epoch in terms of historical relations of human power and exploitation.

Donna Haraway echoes the misconception when she writes that the "sciences of the mid-20th-century 'new evolutionary synthesis' shaped approaches to human-induced mass extinctions and reworldings later named the Anthropocene," before declaring that the Anthropocene has been around "for as long as our species can be identified." She then puts humans firmly in their place, that is, below bacteria as "planetary terraformers."

The cavalier attitude to Earth System science is of a piece with some ecofeminist critiques of science as such. Rather than accept Latour's injunction that the critical urge should aim at *adding* reality to matters of fact,[23] Anna Tsing wants to deprive matters of fact of their reality. She put it bluntly: "It's science – we don't trust it, we don't like it, and we don't want to join. . . . Science, we think, is a form of Man.'[24] Today this kind of attack on science plays only into the hands of the most androcentric of all men, the climate science deniers. Moreover, arguments for human dependence on nature and contemporary criticism of human mastery have mostly originated *in science itself*, especially the ecological sciences.

Post-humanism is constructed on these sciences. The image of the male authority figure using Science to subdue Nature is a dated caricature with little resemblance to the actual world of scientists. Never have C. P. Snow's two worlds been further apart than in the humanities faculties of some American universities.

When post-humanists speak of the Anthropocene the objective is always to dethrone humans, to deny our uniqueness, insisting that we do not stand apart but like everything else are spread through matter living and dead.

> No species, not even our own arrogant one pretending to be good individuals in so-called modern Western scripts, acts alone; assemblages of organic species and of abiotic actors make history, the evolutionary kind and the other kinds too.[25]

 While the urge to counter human arrogance and the misuse of human powers is necessary, the effect of this kind of reduction is to decentralize causality at a time when power has in reality never been more centralized. In this way, anti-anthropocentrism has the perverse effect of *denying* our responsibility for the damage we have caused.

The freak of nature

The arrival of the Anthropocene ought to undermine all theories according to which the distinctions between humans and nature can be dissolved by abolishing the dualisms of modernity and returning to, or adapting, some form of animistic or totemistic unity with nature that would allow us to transcend human chauvinism. Now that the Earth has entered the Anthropocene, and we are obliged to deal with the angry beast we have created, taking the humans-are-just-another-creature standpoint as an actual politics means running, like Dr Frankenstein, from the monster we have created. Or, to be fair, the post-humanists are like Dr Frankenstein's uneasy lab assistants who make themselves scarce at the critical moment, leaving a megalomaniac in sole charge of his monster.

If the Anthropocene brings a message, it is that it's time to accept the obvious: humans stand out from nature as a whole. When *Homo sapiens* appeared there was within it some latent property that, when manifested, caused humans to separate from nature, while always remaining dependent on it. This natural-unnatural creature, the networked super-agent who straddles the realm of necessity and the realm of freedom, can exert enormous influence on nature, even if it cannot control it.

The fundamental lesson of the Anthropocene is this: humans are indeed embedded in nature and in recent decades in the Earth System itself, but the embedding is not a destruction of agency and subjectivity; it constrains them but also allows their fullest expression. So the Anthropocene both undermines dualism *and* reaffirms it, and it does so by showing us that networks do not have to be flat. We need an ontology founded on human-distinctiveness-within-networks rather than an ontology that deprives humans of their unique form of agency. The task now is not to reject the subject–object division but to understand the particular form that subjectivity has taken and what it must become.

Taking the monopoly of agency away from humans, and giving it to non-human and non-living forces or entities, changes the meaning of "agency" so that it no longer means to act with a purpose (as living things do). While agency is always exercised within networks or associations (entanglements that constrain and condition the exercise of subjectivity), collapsing intentionality into an ontological flat-world of influences leaves us bereft of the categories needed to understand power and politics. Alf Hornborg has redeemed agency, while infusing it with added subtlety, by drawing distinctions between non-living objects that have *consequences*, living entities other than humans that have *purposes* (due to their sentience and communication), and humans who have *intentions* (because they can reflect on their purposes). When agency is stripped of all element of choice it becomes mere influence, so we might summarize the distinctions as no choice, choice, and the capacity to make considered choices. Against the idea that agency is distributed across all entities, objects "may constrain, prompt, or mediate the agency of living organisms. But in no case is it justified to dissolve the crucial difference between purposive agency and merely having consequences," not least because in a world in which intentionality has been dissolved into networks or assemblages, there is no power, no freedom, and no morality.[26]

The post-humanist program of taking agency from the human monopoly and allocating it to processes or competing entities took place at exactly the time that in practice humans were accumulating and centralizing so much agency that we now rival the influence of the great forces of nature. In the Anthropocene, the lumpiness of the actual distribution of agency has become *more* pronounced just as post-humanists are telling us that the world is flat. Only in the last two or three decades has the pre-eminence of human agency truly confronted us. No other force, living or dead, is capable of influencing the course of the Earth System *and* has the capacity to decide to do otherwise. Now *that* is agency. It is what makes humans *of* nature but also the freak of nature. The advent of the Anthropocene ought to put to rest both the Moderns' belief in the autonomous subject and the post-humanist insistence that between humans and non-humans there is no sharp difference but only a "gradual continuity."[27] The Anthropocene shows up humans as *super-agents*, powerful even beyond the imaginings of the Moderns, the agent who broke the bounds of Cartesian subjectivity to enter into the object only to find itself confronted by a power over which it can never prevail.

Against the danger of elevating the purified human agent into a different realm, Bruno Latour has inveighed against allowing explicit or implicit controlling forces to rise above the actual world from where they pull the levers, just like the Kantian subject.[28] Warning of the almost universal, if often unconscious, deployment of a two-level standpoint, with disembodied forces like Life, Evolution, Nature, Society, the Market, the System, the Whole, or various other substitutes for God occupying a second level "floating above the first," he insists on sticking to a one-level standpoint from which the real is composed. He strongly defends Lovelock's Gaia idea because that, he says, is what Lovelock intended.

Latour's warning – perhaps the essential insight of his entire *oeuvre* – is profound because it is so hard to internalize. However, if we are to stay with a one-level standpoint then the concentration of agency in humans makes it a topologically uneven level rather than a flat one. If what is outside any entity (its "environment") is indeed "made of forces, actions, entities and ingredients that are flowing through [its] boundaries," then there is one creature that can choose to *resist* the flows and, up to a point, put itself on the "outside."[29] If the Latour procedure is to erase "the distinction between inside and outside of any given entity," the freak of nature is freakish because it is inside *and* outside. In the Anthropocene, both its status as an insider and its status as an outsider have been intensified to an extreme degree.

The ontological wrong turn

For all its "materialism" post-humanism moves in a world of *knowledge*, or rather knowledges and perspectives. It is a reaction against modernity's claim that the only legitimate way to understand the world is through a single universal kind of reason, one that emerged from the foundational distinction between the subject who knows and the object that is known. The "ontological turn" goes beyond post-humanism's defense of different knowledges to defend the truth of a variety of ways of *being*, a plurality of ontologies.

The turn has been lent empirical force from anthropology in the observation that other cultures did not separate and elevate the human in the way the Moderns did. Of course this has been known for a long time. The novel move is to understand these cultures not as alternative ways of *seeing* the world – perspectives interpreted as anything from primitive to respect-worthy to the only means of saving the Earth – but of different worlds, that is, different ways of *being*. The most systematic, powerful and scholarly statement of this position is by Philippe Descola in *Beyond Nature and Culture,* which systematizes ontologies with various combinations of modes of interiority and physicality. He posits four: naturalism (the modern Western way of being), animism (among Amazonian Indians, for example), totemism (Australian Aborigines), and analogism (Chinese geomancy or Europe in the Middle Ages) [30] In this way the Western mode of being is merely one among others, and Descola is not afraid to point to its faults, while maintaining a respectful neutrality toward the other three.

In considering the (Western naturalist) opposition between nature and culture, the non-human and the human, Descola asks which unique feature could separate humans from nature. He concedes that children learn early to distinguish between entities endowed with intentionality and those without it, and that intentionality is only one of a range of obvious differences between oneself and natural objects. Yet, he asks, why draw the frontier between human and object at intentionality or language or the ability to make things? Why not draw the frontier at independence of movement, or at life, or even at material solidity? We Moderns would do better to go to pre-modern ontologies to understand the world around us rather than rely on "the *tiny quantum* by which we distinguish ourselves" from other objects.[31] Well, that tiny quantum was enough to shift the Earth's geological arc and to do so more or less consciously. It was the place at which Moderns stood to move the Earth, and where the lever they used to do it, modern technology wielded by the force of capital accumulation, was manufactured. And the truth is that preventing the Earth from moving a great deal further from its Holocene homeliness cannot be achieved by standing somewhere else, and certainly not in the Amazon rainforest. Or, more accurately, the place to stand must be a step *forward* from the modern one rather than a step backwards.

Descola observes, quite rightly, that nowadays it is hard to refer to any difference between "Us and Others" without being accused of incipient racism (in the case of the bad guys) or "impenitent nostalgia for the past" (in the case of the well-meaning ones).[32] He defends himself from the latter accusation with the argument of his book – that Western cosmology is only one among several ways of being and those immersed in it cannot use it to judge the others (although he in fact does, in a positive way). How am I to defend myself against the accusation of incipient racism when I underscore the difference between modern Us and pre-modern Others? The immediate response is to remind ourselves that Others did not make the Anthropocene; that was done by Us. The implication is, as I have been arguing throughout, that the Moderns are responsible for immense accomplishments by building a system of astonishing dynamism, transforming the conditions of life in ways at once magnificent and ruinous. A second defense is that, notwithstanding all their merits, pre-modern ontologies cannot help us now. While acknowledging the unheralded sophistication of their cosmologies and deep relationships with the natural world, they could not provide the ontological grounding for the vast technological achievements of modernity nor its world-ruining effects.

At the very end of his volume Descola writes that it would be mistaken to think that pre-modern cultures "can bring us a deeper wisdom for the present time than the shaky naturalism of late modernity."[33] Elsewhere he tells us we should not "cling to" our way of seeing the world when there are better ways "still very much alive."[34] But not even the inheritors of those other ways believe that. If we accept the validity of the division of the world into various ways of being and corresponding ontologies, it nevertheless remains true that one of those ontologies, Western naturalism, has become utterly dominant and continues to drive the others from the face of the Earth. This "ontocide" may not succeed completely because Indigenous people, while negotiating their existences in the modern world, are finding means of retaining elements of their cosmologies and ways of being, creating modern-traditional hybrids. At the risk of speaking on their behalf, most Indigenous people understand that old worlds cannot be preserved except by rearticulating them in a dialogue with the modern world. Social scientists who call for a return to non-dualistic premodern ways of being – Descola even suggests we might find dead ones on library shelves and make them "come to life once more'[35] – propose a political strategy that Indigenous people themselves typically do not entertain. So ontological anthropology risks freezing Indigenous people in purified ways of being, whereas they are daily negotiating blends and compromises between modern and non-modern ontologies, not least when engaged in practices such as the production of "traditional" artworks. The new ontological divisions of the avant-garde anthropologists are not worlds that Indigenous people themselves feel obliged to occupy. There are bridges to cross from the modern to the non-modern and back again, and many do it several times a day.

It is true that the grounding of certain Indigenous ontologies holds something that ought to be recovered in a new Anthropocene way of being beyond modernity, and that is their cosmological sensibility. It is the very "primitivity" of these cosmo-ontologies that separates them from more "sophisticated" pre-modern traditions like Christianity, city religions that turned inwards to become preoccupied with the self and its salvation. As the Anthropocene consumes the world, it's hard to listen to earnest words spoken in prayer halls or meditation rooms about how to know God or to achieve emptiness without being struck by the thought that the inwardness of all such journeys of the self serves as a distraction from what is happening outside the window, and that the absence of separation of the traditional Indigenous self from its natural world may hold a powerful message for how to live in the Anthropocene.

Nevertheless, it is not patronizing to say that Indigenous people do not have the solutions to the Anthropocene. The Anthropocene is as much a shock to them as it is to everyone else. To turn to them for answers shoulders them with an impossible burden. We made the mess and "going native" ontologically is no answer. Looking upon Indigenous cultures with awe and regarding them as having magical potency is to fetishize them, a tendency now taken so far by some as to attribute to them the power to fix the climate and reverse the geological destabilization of the planet. There is no need to reject the historical truth of modernity and go looking among pre-modern ontologies for an alternative. The *only way forward* is to begin from where we are, in modernity, and from there work toward a "beyond-modernity" way of being, a fifth ontology to add to Descola's four.

Even if we set all this aside there is a much more compelling reason why it is futile to look to Indigenous ontologies for an answer to the Anthropocene. The vast majority of non-Western people live not in the Amazon rainforests, the Arctic Circle, or the central deserts of Australia; they live in the sprawling cities of China, Nigeria, Brazil, and Indonesia. For the most part, they are quite willing to leave behind the remnants of non-naturalist ontologies – which typically they see anyway as the preserve of primitive tribes within their own territories – and seek to adopt Western ways as quickly as they can. The largest populations of Asia, Latin America, and Africa are attempting, many with extraordinary success, to emulate the growth mania, technological practices, consumer lifestyles, and personal identity formation of the Euro-American way of being. Introducing *Beyond Nature and Culture*, Marshall Sahlins writes that Descola's claim is that "other people's worlds do not revolve around ours." But the hard truth is that in practice they do and, like ours, their worlds are being sucked into the whirlwind of the Anthropocene.

The new great power, China, strives to ensure its best and brightest are steeped in modernity's subject–object ontology by sending them to be shaped by the universities of the North, the cathedral schools of naturalism. If Europe made the transition from the analogism of astrology and alchemy to the naturalism of science across the seventeenth and eighteenth centuries, China has done it in 30 years of industrial growth, albeit on cultural grounds thoroughly tilled, fertilized, and cultivated over the previous four decades by that other great agent of Western naturalism – Marxism. It's too late to exhume the corpse of Confucius.

Neither comparative ontology nor science studies provides a firm basis for social analysis. The preoccupation with objectivity and the "subject–object split" has never extended to the other domains of modernization – business, technology, the state, politics, law, and colonial conquest. Modernity, in the words of Lucas Bessire and David Bond, "has never been organized around any single binary."[36] A mistaken understanding of nature by scientists in their labs was no guide to the messy historical world outside that gave rise to the actual practices of modernity. And against the excessive power attributed to the modern philosophy of culture versus nature, Bessire and Bond remind us that climate change is not due to modernity but to the burning of fossil fuels, and we are better off going to actual history and recent politics to find a way to counter it. One interrogates the nature–culture split in vain for an explanation of why France decided to generate its electricity from zero-emissions nuclear power while Britain took the coal option.

It is a stretch of logic to go from modern science's claim to objectivity to the chauvinism of the anthropologist studying "the savage mind" of the non-Westerner. Those immersed in Western naturalist ontology were not alone in viewing the Other through eyes of racial superiority, as every black person or Korean arriving in nineteenth-century Japan discovered. Cultural chauvinism knows no ontological boundaries. The step from the Moderns seen through science studies to the modernization worldview of the anthropologist – let alone the colonial conqueror – is in fact a large leap. "The Modern" risks becoming a portmanteau into which is stuffed every attitude, practice, and ideology that might be called "Western," one that can be opened up for an answer to any question.

Ostensibly, ontological pluralism has emerged to release us from "the crushing division between Object and Subject."[37] Such a pluralism means we no longer judge other ways of seeing the world through Western eyes, scorning them as superstitious or backward cultures while basking in the light of modernity. But isn't there a third option, other than dismissing pre-modern ontologies as superstition or giving them equal or higher ontological status? It is one that maintains a respectful distance, standing aside and saying "we cannot know, and will not judge," and then acknowledges that Western naturalism emerged supreme, even if it did so merely as the philosophical enabler of European military-technological power and colonial conquest.

" Guns, Germs + Steel "

Recovering the cosmological sense?

When Indigenous people found white invaders on their shores they did not see the occasion as a meaningless accident that "just happened"; they went looking in their cosmologies for an understanding of where the episode fits in their world. Are these white visitors old spirits returning? The sense of grand events embedded in an unfolding order rather than arriving accidentally is characteristic of non-modern cosmologies, and of course to religious traditions in the West. Yet, like humanists, post-humanists understand world history as a series of accidents. A world history purged of all inner meaning is the ontological heart of modern *cosmology*, one captured in the shift in the meaning of the word – from a life-governing set of beliefs about the creation of the world, its meaning, and the place of the tribe within it, to that of theories of the origins and physical structure of the universe.

So a view of modernity as a meaningful unfolding within a larger world or cosmic order is more deeply non-modern than the ontological pluralists' view that it was a historical misfortune to be rectified by going to the ontologies of the non-Moderns to learn how we might merge nature and culture once again or recognize that they never really split. Yet I'm suggesting that, for those who sense some larger meaning in the Anthropocene's arrival and what it may be telling us about the role of humans on Earth, there is no going back to pre-modern ontologies for an understanding; we must look ahead to *the evolution of modernity itself*, driven by its own endogenous forces and contradictions within a larger order.

Recasting agency is at the center of this rethinking. For post-humanists, the human claim to exclusive agency is an illusion. If we are so deeply embedded in networks that the division between humans and non-humans is dissolved and our agency is barely distinguishable from that of an ant or a robot, then intentionality and freedom become mirages. They are suspicious of all categories of early modern philosophy used to define humans as unique creatures – freedom, consciousness, will, Reason. Yet turbo-charged agency was the *essence* of modernity, combining freedom from oppression with power over nature, using science and technology and the institutions that mobilized them.

Yes, post-humanism has taught us to blur the hard-and-fast division between subject and object by accepting our inescapable physical entanglements. It has made us understand, thanks to ecology and Whitehead, that nothing exists outside of its relationships. And it has demolished the idea of capital-S Science rising above the actual world of scientific practice. Yet if humans can exist only within networks that does not mean we are nothing more than nodes in the tangled web of worldly processes. Modernity was not an illusion but the arrival of the time of greatest promise and greatest danger, each represented by real social forces and movements that have fought out the great political and social battles. Only when we accept the greatness of the human project and the extreme danger that goes with it can we pose the epoch-defining question: how are we to use our power to pacify and protect the Earth rather than destroy it?

4 A Planetary History

The significance of humans

It is now common to be reminded of humanity's tenuous place on an insignificant planet in a minor solar system adrift in the vastness of space. Nietzsche expressed it brutally as far back as 1873:

> In some remote corner of the universe, poured out and glittering in innumerable solar systems, there once was a star on which clever animals invented knowledge. ... After nature had drawn a few breaths the star grew cold, and the clever animals had to die.
>
> One might invent such a fable and still not have illustrated sufficiently how wretched, how shadowy and flighty, how aimless and arbitrary, the human intellect appears in nature.[1]

Reprising Nietzsche, Carl Sagan opined that the "only planet we are sure is inhabited is a tiny speck of rock and metal, shining feebly by reflected sunlight, and at this distance utterly lost."[2] These evocations are ventured to shatter the self-importance that always threatens when humans acquire power or believe they are God's chosen creatures. Science played its part in cutting us down to size. As Freud observed, after Copernicus had reduced our planet to a speck in the universe, Darwin turned us into the descendants of monkeys. Freud himself then told us we do not even have control over our conscious minds. When we are reminded that *Homo sapiens* has walked the Earth for a trifling 200,000 of the 3.7 billion years of life on Earth, that human history barely registers on the scale of deep time, and that the Earth is a pinprick in the vastness of the Universe, we are invited to feel inconsequential and to remember our lowly place in the cosmos.

If our existence is inconsequential, our disappearance is meaningless. And so, in response to the clamor to "save the planet," there are those who echo Nietzsche's indifference toward the clever animal that had to die by blithely reminding us that while humans may extinguish themselves, the planet will live on. John Gray captures this mood:

> *Homo rapiens* [*sic*] is only one of very many species, and not obviously worth preserving. Later or sooner, it will become extinct. When it is gone the Earth will recover. ... The earth will forget mankind.[3]

Setting aside the implied cruelty of this kind of statement – its apparent indifference to the scale of the suffering that human extinction would entail through famine, disasters, and war – in truth, if humans were wiped from Earth the planet would not live on, not in any meaningful sense. For *it is we who give the Earth meaning* and mark it out as the unique planet in the cosmos. It is not true, as a poster in the Paris metro warned, that "Nature doesn't need humankind," unless one truly believes both that humans are no different from chimpanzees and that chimps are "not obviously worth preserving." No one really believes either of those, not even pseudo-cynics like Gray, whose statement ought not to be read literally but as a salve applied to turn the pain of exasperation into a more endurable apathy. Yet, unlike the tragedy of the extinction of chimps, the disappearance of human beings would be the profoundest ontological event.

Well-meaning philosophical attempts to instill a sense of humility by cutting humans down to size (the post-humanist strategy) represent a similar belittlement of the great human project – not the project of human domination of the Earth but that of learning how to live wisely, cooperatively, and well within the limits of the Earth, while at the same time cultivating our potentialities and those of the planet. So to suggest that human extinction would be an event of little consequence is the gravest moral error, because it is a repudiation of the human project – the *Earth's* great human project.

If Nietzschean nihilism is unfazed by the end of humans on the planet, the obverse mistake is to deny that the end of humans is possible. One tells us that the tragedy is not a tragedy, the other that the tragedy cannot occur. Such is the stance of the kind of cosmic utopianism of Teilhard de Chardin and Thomas Berry, according to which God or the Universe has a higher plan, one in which the dark side of the human relationship to nature, and so the depredations of the Anthropocene, become a mere phase to be transcended as the plan unfolds.

It is true, as Claude Lévi-Strauss once remarked, that the world began without man and will end without man; yet we now cannot deny that it is man who defines it. *Homo sapiens*, who appeared no more than 200,000 years ago, may disappear from the face of the Earth in the foreseeable future, yet our species' direct influence will endure for hundreds of thousands of years at least and leave an indelible mark. If in a hundred million years' time an alien civilization writes the history of the Universe, the Earth will be known as the Planet of the Humans.

In the face of a warming globe, a new kind of existential defeatism finds expression in the thought, now often voiced, that if humans disappear in the next century or two, then the history of *Homo sapiens* on Earth would be a mere blip in the planet's 10 billion-year history, whose signs would soon be erased by natural processes, and Nature would simply move on. Haraway provides a variation with her characterization of humans as mere compost to be reabsorbed, an earthbound version of the cosmologist's account of human beings as temporary assemblages of cosmic dust. This observation is usually offered up with a wry matter-of-factness that releases the speaker from all concern for the future of the species. Fatalistic acceptance of human extinction is common among post-humanists whose understandable disgust at the brutality of ecological destruction delivers them into a quietism rooted in disavowal of the human project as a whole. The loss of faith in the modern project of freeing humans to allow them to flourish morphs into an unstated judgment (or perhaps Judgment) on the wages of sin, one more resonant with the Old Testament than with the New and its compassion for the fallenness of humankind.

Sister Marion McGillis — The World made conscious.

If humans do end up occupying a mere 200,000 years of the Earth's deep time, it remains true that, in a strong sense, without human beings the Earth could not exist. Its existence would be inconceivable. One can, of course, *picture* it devoid of humans, but only an intelligent being can form such a picture. The human being alone is capable of making worlds on the Earth and so rescuing it from cosmic insignificance. Only humans may turn the Earth into the locus of universal understanding. The extinguishment of humans from the Earth would be a tragedy of cosmic significance.

Does history have a meaning?

As we peer unblinkingly into the Anthropocene future we can hardly resist asking the question: how does this latest stage in the human story fit into the Earth's story? If humans have crossed a threshold to become a geological force, contending with natural forces that operate in deep time, how did we get here? This is not mere causal-chain Big History but an opening into the meaning of history itself. It's a reworking of an ancient question, one that modern science and progress and the philosophies built around them ruled invalid. Yet without a larger conception of humankind, do we not come only to flourish briefly and now destroy the Earth? The struggle – even if lost – to fulfill a larger obligation of responsibility for the Earth might lend direction and meaning to history as a whole. For as we enter the Anthropocene, if human existence is meaningless, then humankind's path to systematic and willful destruction of the conditions of life on Earth is also meaningless. And that, at least for some who reflect on it, scarcely seems possible.

We must, as Nietzsche insisted, face up to the full implications of the "death of God." For him, if we are not the chosen creature, then there is no special meaning to our existence. And yet here we are, in the Anthropocene, a geological epoch brought on by a unique creature with astonishing power. For some there is nothing to explain; that is how it turned out. Sooner or later, though, the nihilistic chickens will come home to roost. Are we really willing to give up on the human story and its almost unimaginable accomplishments, to regard it all as nothing and our existence as a mere assemblage of molecules that came together for a short time to resist entropy? If the modern form of Progress, molded in the Great Acceleration, has brought humankind to the brink of the abyss do we give up on every kind of human advancement? Let me suggest why the answer should be "no."

While modern philosophy abolished all philosophies of history, in practice the belief in Progress as the advance to ever-higher technological and material development became modernity's de facto philosophy of history, one taken up in political ideologies, beginning with Marxism and gradualist counter-moves, including social democracy. Progress now suffuses contemporary thinking so deeply that it no longer qualifies as a belief but constitutes the unnoticed wallpaper of the contemporary world, the "grand narrative" that no longer needs to be recounted, except in exasperated response to certain kinds of ecological critique. Without this secret philosophy of history, which the Anthropocene has now fractured, we seem to be cut adrift. After all, the pressures on each of us to immerse ourselves in the stream of Progress and be swept along by it are almost irresistible. Our freedom then becomes only the liberty to navigate to the left or right side of the current, or, if too weak, sink to the bottom, there to drown. It is true that we are each capable of taking refuge in a quiet eddy, or even clambering out and sitting on the bank, but those who do so find it requires exceptional resolve to resist the lure of the current. The system punishes all resistance; the social pressure is too intense; the anxieties can be overwhelming. Just look at the ridicule and resentment deep greens and voluntary simplifiers attract. It is as if those who crawl out of the stream are betraying an unwritten social compact, betraying history itself.

With the collapse of socialism in 1989, the utopian promise of capitalism mutated into the banal expectation of an ever-expanding present. Yet the official ideology of escalating affluence leaves all but the most obtuse beneficiaries with a nagging sense that there must be something more to it. At the same time, it must strike many that James Lovelock's story of the human species – emerging through a long series of genetic accidents, multiplying and consuming beyond the planet's capacity, and soon to be extinguished by an unfeeling Gaia – is troubling, not just for its indifference to suffering but for its blindness to the manifest uniqueness of human beings. Lovelock's refusal to sentimentalize Gaia is vindicated by Anthropocene science, yet something rebels against the cold acceptance of the canceling out of humankind's immense cultural and intellectual accomplishments. When he conceived of Gaia he seemed simultaneously to consign the human being to the same realm of meaningless existence as cyanobacteria.

And so I would like to pose this question: if the Anthropocene for the first time gave birth to a universal *anthropos*, does the new grand narrative have a backstory, or was its first chapter written in 1945? One can of course understand the advent of the Anthropocene as an accident, the consequence of a sequence of unrelated events devoid of any pattern or thread. Yet it's worth asking whether it can be understood within a broader conception of human and Earth history, not least in order to re-evaluate stories told by powerful thinkers of the past about the inevitable rise of humans to dominate nature, even if they thought in terms of human transformation of the "face of the Earth" rather than the far more hazardous disruption of the Earth System.

After all, we are being asked to face the possibility that humankind will, through our techno-industrial assault on the forces of nature, bring about our own demise. Perhaps the perilous conditions of the Anthropocene draw us toward a new narrative, one that goes beyond description of an increasingly fractious Earth and stressed human societies to suggest a meaning to our place on Earth, a story of humankind that might point to a larger conception of history, a philosophy of history for an *anthropos* that is more than human beings summed into an aggregate. Yet it must be a narrative like no other, for with the transition to the new epoch it cannot be limited to the domain of human history; it must be a *planetary history*, a narrative of human-Earth history.

When philosophers think about the nature of humans, our thinking ability typically becomes the decisive feature – thinking that transcends all embodiment, all embeddedness. Yet is it not the *transformation* of the Earth, rather than the contemplation of it, that accords with humankind's true calling? Whether it follows reflection or not, taking action has given us the Anthropocene. If we are defined merely as thinking beings, then the stupendous changes that humans have wrought on their environments are accidental and not essential to our nature. And yet here we are, in the Anthropocene.

If philosophy can abolish old problems by exposing new conditions, it can also recognize new questions thrown up by those new conditions. I have suggested that for the first time it is legitimate to put forward a narrative of human history as a whole – a world history – since the peoples of the world have been united, willingly or not, by the two late-twentieth-century universalizing forces of globalization and the Anthropocene. It is a narrative that emerges from the immanent structure of the human–Earth relationship and the state it has now assumed. It is a narrative of agency out of control in which human salvation is to be sought neither in the transcendent realm nor in the infinite promises of economic growth, but worked out in practice on Earth by humans together exercising self-restraint.

The prospect of humankind's demise and the ultimate failure of the techno-industrial project sees us disinterring the original human questions – the conundrums of origins, the place of humans on Earth, the meaning of our lives, and salvation. So at the dawn of a new historical epoch it should be no surprise to find ourselves returning to them after three or four hundred secular years in which they were progressively pushed to the margins, and wondering about a narrative that might provide some answers. Before venturing some suggestions, let me make three preliminary observations.

First, if the problem of history coincides with the problem of human existence, the problem of history can never be one of thought alone; it is the history of activity, of striving, of conflict, of achievement, and of failure. If the arrival of the Anthropocene serves as a blunt reminder of the totality of humans as a phenomenon on the Earth, it is by way of our physical impact on the Earth and it is this phenomenon that allows us to create space for a narrative of human–Earth history and a philosophy of geohistory. So to open up the question of the nature of humans and their story is not a call for greater introspection in search of the structures of Reason or states of consciousness. To go looking on the inside for answers to a problem that is so manifestly on the outside can now be seen as a modern form of evasion. It calls instead for extended reflection, informed by the evidence of Earth System science, on what it means for humanity to have arrived at the predicament of the Anthropocene. It is the Anthropocene that finally allows a clear view of what humans truly are.

Second, the difference between the old stories and the new one is more than scientific, that is, more than a rewrite to "take account of the environment," or even of Earth System science. The new story has a new main character, no longer the protagonist of modernity, the autonomous subject blessed with consciousness and reason and so the capacity to decide. The newborn *anthropos* is a conception centered on humankind's world-making practices, the power to shift the Earth, for good or ill. We might speak of the transformation of humankind into the shackled super-agent, torn between two irresistible forces – a self-assertion that, convinced of its independence, aspires to transcend all boundaries, but which is up against the limits imposed by an Earth that remains implacable and ever-more recalcitrant.

Third, it's no longer tenable to imagine a divine agent directing events toward a predetermined goal; but that is not to say that events are not pushed toward an end by laws, forces, or tendencies internal to the system, that is, a *teleonomy* of processes that gives direction without intention, end-directed without being end-seeking. Self-organizing systems always have a tendency; they act *as if* they have an intended result. And is it not reasonable to think that the drive that saw humans spread across the Earth and increasingly transform the environment could at some stage become so large and active that it would rival some of the great forces of nature? It was not inevitable, for there were countervailing forces restraining thoughtless exploitation of nature, from the Romantics to the modern environmental movement in all of its variations. Yet the propensity to end up where we are was strong enough to give rise to a legitimate sense of directionality in the history of human–Earth relations.

An Enlightenment fable

So let me tell a fable about the destiny of humans on Earth that might explain the sense of directionality in human–Earth relations prompted by the arrival of the Anthropocene. The fable might go like this. Three to four centuries ago, after a much longer period of preparation, humankind embarked on the second last phase of the "hazardous adventure in individual freedom."[4] Ceded the power to make worlds that transform the Earth, and therefore capable of taking responsibility for it, humans stood before an open vista that promised the fulfillment of our destiny, the opportunity to find our true mission. If the death of God saw the defeat of the individual preoccupation with salvation and damnation, humankind was at the same time born into the role of master of its own destiny. And the essential question became whether it would attempt to make worlds that defy the constraints of the Earth or make worlds in which nature flourishes too, that is, worlds in which humankind takes responsibility for the Earth's healthy evolution. This was the ultimate historical contingency opened up by modernity.

Having fulfilled its task of creating free beings with enormous potential for power over nature while always subject to its constraints, destiny withdrew so that men and women could chart their own course on Earth, developing their powers and choosing to embrace responsibility or abjure it. Those for whom God lived on would have to act *etsi deus non daretur*, as if there were no God. Would we use our freedom to find a way concordant with our possibilities? Would we attempt to defy fate or collaborate with it? The dawning of freedom, and especially the freedom to transform nature, was the condition that opened up this question. From that point, if our destiny were to be known it could not be read from holy books but from our own understanding of the world and its history. Destiny would not impose itself upon us but allow us the freedom to choose – to live with abandon or accept the duty to care for the Earth. And ourselves: the possibility of nuclear annihilation has kept humans on the precipice of existence.

To express the fable's set-up a little differently: destiny's hand became hidden to enable us to "forget" it, directing our attention elsewhere, to treat events as accidental or the outcomes of our own free choices. Separated from nature but preoccupied with understanding and mastering it, our consciousness became concentrated inwards on ourselves and our plans, including winning the maximum amount of autonomy. Yet the "hidden hand" of our larger role on Earth remained available to knowledge for those sensitive to the signs, now unmistakable in the stunning facts of the Anthropocene. There always remained a faintly audible drumbeat of something larger, some purpose beyond our daily attempts to get ahead. It was not to be heard the old way, through numinous experience, but through the process of worldly observation and understanding, discernible in the movement of human and Earth history.

The path to realizing our destiny was no longer a spiritual journey but an intellectual and physical one, building on the "epistemic distance" opened up by the scientific worldview. Ultimately, however, it was a power struggle between contending social forces, the forces of neglect – power-hunger, greed, growth fetishism, hedonism, and psychological weaknesses – against the forces of care: self-restraint, respect for the natural world, love of one's children, and the desire for civilization to flourish.

Put in somewhat different terms, the story is that Earth and humans are still in the process of creation and our pre-eminent task is to achieve a reconciliation with the Earth at a time when we have an advanced understanding of its workings and, for good or ill, the power to change its course. So humankind was born into the world in an underdeveloped intellectual and moral state with a mission to achieve maturity by learning to live on and transform the Earth conscientiously. Maturity could only become possible once we had our freedom, once the world had come of age, for whatever path we take must be freely chosen. Just as there is no good without evil, to choose to care for the Earth is possible only if we can equally choose to neglect it. Thus the question of how to live with the Earth could ultimately be resolved only after we had developed the power to destroy life on it. Only in such an environment could humanity succeed in attaining full moral development – or fail to do so, as the case may be.

After the disenchantment of the Earth – the withdrawal of soul as nature was subjected to the power of scientific knowledge – we had the opportunity to develop a relationship of responsible care and so rise to our full possibilities as moral beings, accepting the greater duty for nature that accrues with each leap in our autonomy from it. Without the separation, while human consciousness remained immersed in nature, free of the temptations to neglect and exploit her, there could be no struggle to find the right path. But after nature's disenchantment and God's withdrawal, the search began for a new justification for human existence. The struggle to learn how to live collectively on the Earth and within its limits is *the way*, the opportunity for humankind to find its place in the cosmos.

Some readers may recognize structural similarities between the fable I have just told and what is known as the "Irenaean theodicy." Named for the second-century Church father Irenaeus, his was a theology that lost out to the harsher one of Augustine, although a form of Irenaean theodicy lives on in Eastern Orthodoxy.[5] Irenaeus contended that, rather than arriving on Earth in a perfected state only to be sullied by temptation in the Garden of Eden, man is in a process of creation. The "original sin" should be regarded not as a permanent and debilitating stain but as a childhood lapse; the true contest between good and evil remained to be staged after we had matured and became *free* to make autonomous decisions.

Only through our own moral efforts may we become perfected persons. It was a theology foreseeing a process in which human beings would develop, under God's guidance, into autonomous creatures able to choose good over the temptations of evil.

The secular fable I have ventured mirrors the broad Irenaean structure in which humans must *evolve* into beings able to exercise full moral autonomy and the power to transform the world for good or ill, to exercise their world-shaping responsibility with care or neglect. As in the Irenaean theodicy, the "Fall" did not occur in the garden of man's birth; it is an event still unfolding and with the outcome uncertain. The uncertainty of the outcome distinguishes the "anthropodicy" offered here from that of the ecomoderns. For them, man mirrors God in his benevolence and omnipotence; for me, man is Shakespeare's man, both glorious and tragic, for whom benevolence is what is at stake and the aspiration to omnipotence is the most dangerous temptation.

If we succumb to the temptation, as we appear to have, the future historians of the cosmos will identify the century after World War II, and particularly the decades from the 1990s when we knew what we were doing, as the time of the Fall. In this story the primal sin is not to defy God's command but to misuse the gift of our special agency by violating the Earth, destroying the home provided to us.

Irenaeus could not have imagined the immense power over the material world that humans would develop and the temptations that go with such power. Moreover, the dilemma is not a personal moral struggle against evil that would settle the fate of the individual, but one for humankind. Whatever virtue the individual may accrue by treading lightly on the Earth, the power to

126

destroy can only be controlled collectively because the choice to be made is one for the system – for structures, institutions, and cultures, dominated by the powerful but subject to change by a determined populace.

For Irenaeus, although man must grow to maturity before truly facing the temptations of evil, it is always implicit that good will ultimately prevail. So when granting self-determination to man God rigged the race to ensure his preferred outcome. In a world where the decisive question is no longer one of personal salvation but common responsibility for the Earth, the outcome cannot be predetermined but is fully an act of collective will whose end has always been uncertain, even now when the forces of neglect have the upper hand. With the advent of the Anthropocene it is apparent just how we chose to use our autonomy.

"Politics is fate"

When asked about human destiny, Will Self snorted: "We don't speak of the destiny of molluscs, so what is different about humans?" Self was denying the ontological distinction between molluscs and humans, while sitting on a stage in front of an attentive audience at a writers' festival reflecting on the meaning of the existence of the species, which seems enough to tell us that the meaning of human existence bears no comparison with that of the oyster, or even the chimpanzee, and that the idea of human destiny may be worth taking seriously. So let me make some speculations, and they are no more than that, as to what the arrival of the Anthropocene suggests about human destiny.

The climate crisis and the advent of the Anthropocene are disclosing something new and fundamental. From a planetary historical standpoint, we can see the Anthropocene not merely as an event that happens to humans and transforms them, and not simply as an age that humans brought about. We are immersed in the Earth's flows, because human will, or its effects, now merge with the natural forces that govern the Earth's evolution. We are drawn to see it as an ontological shift in the history of the Earth, one in which the secular goal of human perfectibility must be relinquished and the technological will to power must be transcended – willingly or by *force majeure*.

It is no longer tenable to make the humanist assumption that the future is made by humanity alone. At the same time, if we stay with a purely scientific conception of the Earth not much of interest can be said and we are left searching for a way to comprehend the meaning of the turning point that has arrived in human history and in Earth history. We are shifting from humanist history as the story written by free humans to geohistory, a story penned by geohistorians, attempting to tell the story of powerful beings soon to be overwhelmed by more powerful forces. After Chakrabarty's seminal observation that when humans became a geological force the distinction between natural history and human history collapsed, and in the light cast by Latour's reimagination of Gaia,[6] E. H. Carr's famous demarcation of history must not so much be discarded but reversed.

> History begins when men begin to think of the passage of time in terms not of natural processes – the cycle of the seasons, the human life-span – but of a series of specific

events in which men are consciously involved and which they can consciously influence.[7]

Historical studies are studies of agents acting in an unconscious natural world that carries on regardless. Now, our future has become entangled with that of the Earth's geological evolution. From here on, our history will increasingly be dominated by "natural" processes influenced by humans, injected with agency but increasingly beyond our control because the Earth is becoming less controllable in the Anthropocene. It is not, of course, the end of human agency; but in contrast to modernity's infinite horizon of possibility we enter an epoch of narrowing limits to agency. Contrary to the modernist faith, it can no longer be maintained that humans make their own history, for the stage on which we make it has now entered into the play as a dynamic and capricious force. The social sciences taught in our universities – including those that "take the environment into account" – must now be regarded as Holocene disciplines. The process of reinventing them – so that what is taught in arts faculties is true to what has emerged in science faculties – will be a sustained and arduous intellectual enterprise.

What is unique and startling about the science of the Anthropocene is that by definition the new geological epoch cannot be separated from the activities of free humans. Earth System science is the first science to arise from the merging of the realm of necessity and the realm of freedom. It can give us knowledge of the Earth System but it cannot, taken alone, give us knowledge of the larger implications of the Anthropocene. For that we need philosophy.

For those in the tradition of Hegel and Marx, history is a self-completing process unfolding toward a final state, moving inexorably toward the realization of Spirit, a classless society, or indeed liberal capitalism's universal affluence. The idea of freedom is transformed into one that must reconcile itself to some Law of Progress. The problem that bedeviled early modern philosophy, the contradiction between freedom and necessity, is simply transcended. If history is the story of human progress toward ever-greater fulfillment, self-determination, and prosperity – albeit with lapses and detours along the way – the pull of history robs freedom of its openness.

Here, at a time when the necessity of nature is reasserting itself, I am calling for a historical conception that enables the freedom of indeterminacy, allowing a purer freedom within tighter constraints. It's not an argument for substituting speculative history for actual history but seeks to find, within a material understanding of history, a sense of the meaning of the actual unfolding of events. This kind of retroactivity, in which things "will have been" necessary, seems strange, as it goes against the grain of linear causality and the idea that there is a sufficient cause for the occurrence of every event. It seeks *reasons* as well as causes, reasons and causes that, in Slavoj Žižek's words, "are retroactively activated by what is, within the linear order, their effect."[8]

If, as Žižek writes, "the eminently 'historical' moments are those marked by great collisions in which a whole form of life is threatened, when the established social and cultural norms no longer guarantee a minimum of stability and cohesion," there can be no greater collision than the one now taking place between human history and Earth history.[9] Opening ourselves up to the end of our ability to control our common fate – which is, after all, the inner meaning of Anthropocene science – marks the end of the modern era. The conviction that we can use technology to ward off the disruption and wind back the geological clock misunderstands the arrival of the new epoch because the fate of the Earth and the fate of humans are now fused. What we, under duress, are called on to do is combine freedom with responsibility, to ground the realm of freedom in the realm of necessity, and accept the consequences.

Nor should our thinking be limited to a concern with the events of the past. To grasp the meaning of the new epoch we must project ourselves into the thinking of the future, to bring it into the present so that history is not limited to the past. If the Enlightenment was not just a happening that humans stumbled into or an event that humans constructed out of the circumstances in which they found themselves, but was indeed the event that began the period of humanity's coming of age, then the Anthropocene is the disclosure that brings to an end the coming of age and inaugurates the age of consequences in our bid for adulthood. Our past becomes comprehensible in the light cast by the sudden constellation of forces expressed in "the Anthropocene," the closing of the age of openness with the triggering of now-unstoppable disturbances to the functioning of the Earth System.

The arrival of the historical juncture of the Anthropocene allows us to look on the past in a new way. We see the blossoming of freedom in the Enlightenment and then the scientific-industrial revolution no longer as the beginning of the last and permanent stage of humankind, the final maturation of civilization. Instead we understand it as the dawn of the era of responsibility, of the challenge of working out how humans could fulfill their potential and live on the Earth at the same time. The ironic twist was that the humans who woke to this dawn did so with a belief, seemingly justified, that their powers, like their appetites, had no limit. The test was to come to understand that the world is one of limits and that this understanding must be internalized as a set of duties, the obligation to exercise the newfound power respectfully and judiciously. It was the uncertain outcome of this test that left the fate of humans and the Earth open. Now, however, in the Anthropocene the fate of one determines the fate of the other and it is within this dangerous alliance that clues to human destiny may be found.

If for those of a conservative disposition the historical sense is, in T. S. Eliot's words, "a perception, not only of the pastness of the past, but of its presence,"[10] then in the Anthropocene we may say that the present is drenched with the future, bringing a feeling for humanity's whole future, the unsettling presence of times to come. With its outlines now discernible, if only dimly, the future is no longer an undetermined domain to which one can escape by means of techno-utopian dreaming – climate engineering, the singularity, terraforming, space travel, and so on. Conservatism's defense of the value of pastness, including the virtue of rooting subjectivity in something more stable than the whims of the present, cannot survive in an epoch in which the future presses so insistently on us. Catherine Malabou writes of "the anticipatory structure operating within subjectivity itself," a structure that means both seeing what is coming and "not knowing what is coming," except that now the future is one of thwarted dreams. For those now alert to the arrival of the Anthropocene, this *voir venir* represents, more concretely than she imagined, "the interplay of teleological necessity and surprise."[11] We know what is coming, but we do not know its precise delineations; the Anthropocene will surprise us again and again because it marks a shift in the Earth from predictability to volatility.

The past looms as large for radicals as for conservatives, but for the logic of rupture rather than continuity, even if we now see that their ruptures always assumed the continuity of the Holocene. For Hegel and Marx, the past was the ground for the trajectory of the future; its horrors, while not forgiven, would be redeemed so far as they were "necessary" for bringing the realization of the final state. No God appearing as *deus ex machina*, no divine intercession, would be required for the realization; the future is enfolded into the past. In practice, what they assumed to be continuous has been disrupted; and the speculative future thought to play in the present has become a physical one.

The science of the Anthropocene inverts Karl Barth's view of the impossibility of knowing the world of the Last Judgment: "We ... do not know what Nature, as the cosmos in which we have lived and still live here and now, will be for us then; what the constellations, the sea, the broad valleys and heights, which we see and know now, will say and mean then."[12] Gazing at the scientists' colour-coded thermal maps of what the Earth will look like a century hence, with much hotter regions glowing red and much drier ones wilting in yellow, we can indeed make out, through the haze of residual uncertainty, the broad contours of nature under the influence of this new human power.

The super-agent had the choice to care for the Earth or neglect it. The emergence of modern liberties combined with the accumulation of technological power were the conditions for the actual manifestation of the care–neglect polarity, a world of contingency in which the choice would be forced upon us. Modernity came to see this kind of polarity resolved through the superior upward thrust of Progress in the form of economic growth. As it turned out, there were forces that would contain the upward thrust of Progress, forces that would drag it down.

The contention that freedom turbocharged by technology came into being as the freedom to care for or neglect the Earth contradicts all narratives of endless human progress built on expanding control of our environments, of freeing ourselves from the contingency and fractiousness of nature. The belief that when humans gain sufficient freedom from material want they will choose to care for that which sustains them appears to be, with the Anthropocene upon us, little more than an economists' fantasy, the kind of wishful thinking that grants permission for continued destruction. Perhaps, if we had tempered belief in our own rationality with an acceptance of the possibility of wanton neglect, it would not have been necessary for the Earth to remind us so resoundingly of the one-sidedness of our decision.

Against the temptation to construe the history of the world in terms of metaphysical forces, we might recall Napoleon's words to Goethe: "Politics is fate."[13] While modernity was intoxicated by the promise of total liberation, now we see that the paramount question would be what we would *do* with our freedom. Freedom is not the greatest thing; how we decide to use our freedom is the greatest thing. So out of political and economic changes that gave humans enough power and discretion to transform the Earth arose *the choice*. The forces bearing on the choice, for responsibility or for neglect, were concrete historical ones. As I have said, on the side of responsibility are gathered the armies of scientific insight into Earth's physical limits, evidence of the harms caused by actual ecological disruption, the logic of long-term self-interest, the political power of environmentalism, an inner attachment to the beauty and integrity of nature, and a sense in some cultures and religions that we have an obligation to protect the creation. Against these, neglect mobilized the armies of avarice intrinsic to an economic structure driven by the profit motive, the enormous political power of corporate interests, the seemingly insatiable demand for material affluence, along with the human weaknesses of willful ignorance, apathy, evasion, and denial. Can more be said *philosophically* about this titanic struggle over how to use our agency?

5 The Rise and Fall of the Super-agent

Freedom is woven into nature

The decisive act of modernity, according to the philosophical fathers of the age, was that of a man sweeping away the fog of medieval obscurantism to discover the liberatory power of pure reason. With this act, humankind embarked on a historical enterprise in which we could flourish fully for the first time. In his foundational essay of 1784, "What Is Enlightenment?," Immanuel Kant argued that freedom – freedom to make public use of our reason – arose because humans found the fortitude to seize it and to take the path of self-determination instead of subjecting ourselves to the vagaries of divine salvation. In short, we left our adolescence behind and attained our majority. The history of human freedom, in this narrative, was a fortuitous happening that followed a spontaneous outbreak of intellectual courage on the part of a handful of free thinkers.

If modernity was an era in which humankind had to ground itself afresh and make ourselves subject to our own moral law, the secure place from which we did so was the certainty of our own understanding, that is, Descartes' inner domain of "clarity and distinctness." In so doing, we extracted ourselves from the forces surrounding us, not only those of religious superstition but also from an "enchanted" nature, giving rise to a mechanical universe overseen by a distant god. Nature was rendered inert and passive. A dead world was unthinkable in pre-modern times, when "Soul flooded the whole of existence and encountered itself in all things,"[1] and miners performed propitiatory rituals before digging into the living earth.

How we understand the primordial act of modernity frames how we respond to the event of the Anthropocene, surely one of equal moment to the arrival of modernity or, indeed, of civilization itself. If it was a fortuitous act of self-liberation achieved by the clever animal, *animal rationalis*, then we owe our liberty to nothing and are free to use it as we please. Our sovereignty makes no demands on us. Yet even as this new view of man emerged, in the shadows another understanding formed, one that now comes into the light with the arrival of the Anthropocene. What if human freedom were not a random *epiphenomenon* snatched from nature by a few courageous philosophers who fashioned a "realm of freedom" in opposition to the hitherto omnipresent "realm of necessity"? What if freedom belongs to nature-as-a-whole so that, in Friedrich Schelling's thought, *freedom is woven into the fabric of nature*?[2] Such an idea appeals to those who sense that life and human existence are not mere accidents. It gains empirical force when we no longer think of the Earth as an elaborate mechanism subject only to mathematical laws of cause and effect but as a self-organizing dynamic system characterized by *emergent properties* in the way contemporary science itself tells us. Emergent properties belong to the system but cannot be found in any individual element of it and evade all cause-and-effect explanations. In such systems – and the Earth System is the mother of them all – the future always evades full predictability and inevitably holds surprises.

Before scientists began to understand self-organizing complex systems and the spontaneous creativity that characterizes them, the fact of creation, including the creation of life, had to be either attributed to divine intervention or somehow crunched into a cause-and-effect mechanism. For the religiously inclined, nature's spontaneous creativity might be the last redoubt for God, and a pretty good one as it's immune to the embarrassments that the "God of gaps" had to endure as scientific explanation filled one gap after another. It may also be the source of Attenborough-like wonderment at nature's extraordinary ingenuity and limitless generative power.

The spontaneity of freedom makes sense within a complex system with emergent properties. It is consistent with the kind of planet that Earth System science is beginning to reveal and explain to us, one capable of naively giving rise to life, and then intelligent life. Such an understanding suggests a resolution of the apparent contradiction between our *actual separation* from nature and our *unshakable dependence* on it. If freedom is woven into nature-as-a-whole, then that is only the obverse of the idea of the embedded subject, for whom nature is woven into freedom. This thought provides not only a philosophical basis for the Anthropocene's melding of the human and the natural, but also opens up space for an ethics that is neither exclusively inter-subjective nor buried in nature, but begins with a subjectivity that can never wrench itself free of its material roots.

Critics of subjectivist philosophies have always sought to overcome them by endeavoring to integrate discursive thought with intuitive or sensual knowledge.[3] Yet from where we stand now, the critics were hamstrung because they began on the same subjectivist ground and only attempted to expand *forms of knowledge*, even if the other kind of knowledge was said to come from somewhere else (the numinous or the noumenon). Now we see that the Kantian categories of subject and object have collapsed. With the arrival of Anthropocene Earth freedom/spontaneity can no longer be allocated to the domain of the subject and necessity is no longer owned by the object/nature.

If the definitive Kantian division of the world between the realm of necessity (nature and its laws) and the realm of freedom (occupied by man) seems to be of philosophical interest only, it is in fact the essence of modernity.[4] It is how we, in an unconscious and quotidian way, define ourselves – as isolated egos existing inside bodies distinct from the world around us. However, the "free man" born of modernity now discovers that he is bonded and bounded in a completely new way – no longer simply "dependent on his environment," instead inhabiting a realm that is not the passive stage on which he can act out his freedom but a world animated, unruly, and irritable. Before the arrival of the Anthropocene, it was possible to believe in the bifurcated Kantian structure of the modern world; since its arrival, the two realms have bled into one another. Freedom is restricted and conditional and must be played out tentatively on a disorderly and reactive Earth. Necessity is unpredictable and intemperate, liable to overreact to the proddings of free beings. This is why the first objective of this book has been to begin the task of reinventing freedom and necessity in the light of our new knowledge of the Earth System.

The work of the "postologists" – especially Bruno Latour, but also Haraway, Tsing, and Isabelle Stengers, among others – succeeded in breaking down the Kantian division, enmeshing the two realms by redistributing agency and exposing the unsustainability of the human monopoly on freedom. What they could not foresee was that, with the arrival of the Anthropocene, deconstructed freedom had to be reconstructed, this time as an *anthropos* centered around its unprecedented power, an *anthropos* that gathered so much agency that it came to rival the great forces of nature, only to discover it was a freedom tightly bound by a wild and defiant realm of necessity, with its own "agency" that exceeds ours.

The peril of our times is that human beings have yet to realize that freedom can no longer operate independently of necessity, and so continue to act as Moderns, free to play out their agency on a compliant Earth.

If we acknowledge the Earth System's emergent properties – its capacity for spontaneous creativity – then the realm of freedom was always a latent possibility within nature. In this free creature, however, the Earth gave birth to a stubborn child who grew to maturity at times convinced he could break all bonds and lord it over the matrix that generated him. Such an understanding (one implicit in the fable I related in the previous chapter) allows for the existence of the particular *anthropos* of the new anthropocentrism, the powerful world-making creature whose worlds are always circumscribed and immersed in the actuality of the agents' embodiment, and so their embeddedness in the natural world.

This conception of freedom as woven into nature is both more and less anthropocentric than the Kantian one. It is *less* because freedom is forever folded into nature and not conjured into existence by bold thinkers using their own brainpower. The possibility of freedom always resided in nature and once manifested must be bound to it, networked into nature. It is *more* because knowing freedom's source within nature-as-a-whole comes with a heavy responsibility, to protect and enhance nature, to live within its limits as we make new worlds. In other words, it brings an ethics that *begins* with our duties to the "object" and only then to other subjects, an ethics that like all others springs from the freedom to choose, but unlike others must be rooted in the realm of necessity. If freedom is woven into nature, then responsibility too is woven into nature.

In the light of this new double crossing from human to nature, from necessity back to freedom, humankind is no longer the anomaly, the freak of nature. We become *the key* to nature-as-a-whole. Certainly, the injection of human will into the functioning of the Earth System in the Anthropocene becomes more intelligible if freedom is somehow made intelligible in nature-as-a-whole. In that case, our activities in bringing on a new epoch in the geohistory of the planet should not be regarded only as an ethical lapse, with no function in the unfolding of nature-as-a-whole; they tell us something fundamental about the nature of the whole and the arc of its narrative. Yet if humans become the key to nature-as-a-whole it is not in the sense of the mystical traditions, captured in Schopenhauer's aphorism: "We must learn to understand nature from ourselves, not ourselves from nature."[5] Schopenhauer was restating the first lesson of the "perennial philosophy": since each being contains within it the essence of the whole world, the All can be found within if one knows how to find it. In such an understanding, the only form of advance is to higher states of consciousness. In the arc of geohistory revealed by the Anthropocene, however, the dynamic belongs to the changing material relationship of free beings with the Earth, and chasing higher states of consciousness becomes a form of avoidance.

If the Anthropocene represents the convergence of human history and geological history, nature-as-a-whole is the domain in which both move so that they *can* converge. The new epoch forces us to acknowledge the dynamic reciprocity of humankind and Earth, the "synthesis of history and nature," both of which belong to a totality, a whole that is trans-historical in the sense that all history takes place within it. While Schelling saw this synthesis as "the symbol of eternal unity,"[6] in practice it turns out not to be a harmonious marriage between humans and nature but a conjugal war in which neither is able to divorce the other. If nature desired to dissociate itself from humans it would find it had made a creature of great tenacity and resourcefulness. And the only way humans could divorce themselves from nature would be to depart the planet forever, a dream on which I will have more to say.

If anyone wished to challenge the marriage's existence then the arrival of a new stage in geohistory, blending human will with geological processes, must dispel all doubt. The fact that we are now able to recognize this implicates us and our world-making capability more deeply in the totality. If humans are the "unnatural" creatures by way of a world-making propensity that puts us partly outside the lawfulness of nature, then the totality must encompass the unnatural and the natural as one, even if today a great struggle is taking place between the forces of nature and unruly humans, a struggle in which nature responds with growing irritability.

The Anthropocene brings philosophy back to the sensual world, the world of experience rather than thinking – of world creation on a material foundation, of striving, of neglect and care, of natural limits. It is philosophy immersed in the flux of actual life instead of the abstract rules of the analytical mind. It means the privileging of questions of our being, of our nature, before questions of knowledge. In the philosophies of knowledge nature became subsidiary, allowing, in Bruce Matthews's words, "an inflation of the cogito that leads to the vainglorious deification of the human subject" at the cost of the "annihilation of nature."[7] It is no wonder that mainstream ethics today, preserved in the formaldehyde of purified subjectivity, has nothing to say about the Anthropocene.

Schelling was perhaps the first to argue, around 1800, that the rise of subjectivism and its split of the thinking subject from nature provide the theoretical justification for the destruction of nature. But that cannot be the whole story. One cannot reject modernity's actual distancing from nature as such, but only challenge the *form* it took. In the world come of age, it is not our *split* from nature that must be overcome, but our violence against it, arising from the conviction that the split was a total severance. It is better to say that the rise of subjectivism opened up the *possibility* of the actual destruction of nature, but it also opened up resistance to it. Opposition to the depredations of industrialism was present from the outset, and subjectivism as philosophy and as mode of consciousness gave rise to modern politics itself, including a politics that challenges the dominant form of subjectivism. If returning to a pre-modern mode of consciousness is neither possible nor desirable, a new anthropocentrism emanating from the embedded subject is the only way into the future.

So when humankind came of age we had a *choice*. We could decide how to use our turbocharged agency – the freedom whose capacity for good or ill was multiplied a thousandfold by the liberation of our creativity in the course of the scientific-industrial revolution. More than this, I claim that the coming of age was not an accident, or an event triggered by a few intrepid men, or the inexorable evolution of a process in train for millennia. Our coming of age was the manifestation of the agency latent in nature-as-a-whole, when humans, alone in a disenchanted world from which the gods had withdrawn, were ceded the opportunity to earn the right to "inherit the Earth." The concentration of agency in humans is not without meaning; freedom with Earth-changing power put us in the position where we had to decide how humans could flourish without destroying the Earth.

Humanity's creative powers embody the possibility that they be used to *enhance* the life-enriching potential of the Earth as well as to improve the human condition. Nature therefore contains within it the possibility of mutually harmonious human–Earth enhancement. One might say, speaking teleonomy rather than teleology, that when humankind emerged the Earth was generating a being who could enhance it to reveal its extraordinary possibilities, including the cultivation of the cultural, intellectual, and moral powers of humankind itself, a creature with the potential to become the most sophisticated being, able to reflect on nature and comprehend it in new ways, as well as to transform it.

Human agency is not freedom for freedom's sake, power for power's sake, or merely the means to human well-being and material growth. It is much bigger than that, for beyond all purely human-oriented aspirations must be the cultivation of our relationship with the planet to the enduring benefit of both. Indeed, pursuit of the human good, taken in isolation, gives rise to meaninglessness. A conception of the responsible cultivation of the Earth fends off the dragon of nihilism that stalks every society once it attains a moderate level of affluence and peace. For if humans are free to set their own ends and they set ends that are their own, attaining them leaves nothing, other than a yearning for something else. The duty to care for the Earth is the *meaningful* goal as well as the prudent one. So the question is not only whether freedom will be used to advance the common good of humans (for humanity to set its own ends), but whether those ends will be set to include the protection and enhancement of the life-sustaining capacities of the natural world. In other words, rather than history circling around the question of human advancement, we now discover that all along it was not so much conflict between human beings that put all greater dreams in jeopardy; it was conflict with nature that would prove decisive.

Responsibility is not enough

We humans are adept at avoiding responsibility. The proposal to cool the Earth by coating it with a layer of sulphate aerosols to reduce the amount of incoming solar radiation is the technofix to end all technofixes, a grand technological intervention that would side-step the awkward "socio-fixes" demanded by continued emissions of greenhouse gases. Rather than slashing the asset value of some of the globe's biggest corporations, asking consumers to change their habits, or imposing unpopular taxes on petrol and coal, this form of solar geoengineering carries the implicit promise that it will protect the prevailing politico-economic system, which is why certain conservative American think tanks that for years have attacked climate science as fraudulent have endorsed geoengineering as a promising response to global warming.[8] It not only protects the system but vindicates it in the face of criticism from environmentalists, for it would prove that any problem, even one as big as climate change, can be solved by human ingenuity and a can-do attitude. At least, it would if it worked. Doubts that the Earth System would collaborate in any intervention to take control of the climate system and regulate it to suit human needs are well founded in Earth System science.

Solar geoengineering is no fantasy; a fleet of planes packed with sulphates could feasibly be deployed within the next few years. Another kind of grand techno-savior will take several decades. Plans are afoot to escape the ecological mess by fleeing into space. In 2014 we read in *The Times*:

> British scientists and architects are working on plans for a "living spaceship" like an interstellar Noah's Ark that will launch in 100 years' time to carry humans away from a dying Earth.[9]

Known as Project Persephone – curious because in Greek mythology Persephone was the queen of the dead – its website announces that the goal is to build "prototype exovivaria – closed ecosystems inside satellites, to be maintained from Earth telebotically, and democratically governed by a global community."[10] NASA and DARPA, the US Defense Department's advanced technologies agency, are also developing a "worldship" designed to take a multi-generational community of humans beyond the solar system.

Paul Tillich once noted the intoxicating appeal space travel holds for certain kinds of people. The first space flights became symbols of a new ideal of human existence, "the image of the man who looks down at the earth, not from heaven, but from a cosmic sphere above the earth."[11] If Project Persephone's avatars dream big, a reader of the *Daily Mail* brings it down to earth: "Only the 'elite' will go. The rest of us will be left to die."

Perhaps being left to die on the home planet would be a more welcome fate. Imagine being trapped on this "exovivarium," a self-contained world in which exported nature becomes a tool for human survival, a world where there is no night and day, no seasons, no mountains, streams or oceans, no worms or wedge-tailed eagles, no ice, no storms, no winds, no sky, no Sun, a closed world whose occupants would work to keep alive by simulation the archetypal habits of life on Earth. What kind of person imagines him or herself living in such a world? What kind of being, after some decades, would such a post-terrestrial realm create? What kind of children would be bred there?

According to Project Persephone's sociologist, Steve Fuller: "If the Earth ends up *a no-go zone for human beings* due to climate change or nuclear or biological warfare, we have to preserve human civilization."[12] But *why* would we have to preserve human civilization? What is the value of a civilization if not to raise human beings to a higher level of intellectual sophistication and moral responsibility? What is a civilization worth if it cannot protect the natural conditions that gave birth to it? Those who fly off leaving behind a ruined Earth would carry into space a fallen civilization. As the Earth receded into the all-consuming blackness, those who looked back on it would be the beings who had shirked their most primordial responsibility, beings corroded by nostalgia and survivor guilt.

For those who refuse to shirk responsibility for the Anthropocene, what guidance can we draw from the traditions of justice and ethics? When we step back and survey the epoch-stopping force of anthropogenic climate change and mass extinctions our established ethical categories and legal principles appear banal and feeble. If the human impact has been so powerful that it has deflected the Earth from its natural geological path, describing the state of affairs as "unethical" or "unlawful" seems to be some kind of category error. Penal codes proscribe offenses against property and the person. Some codify crimes against humanity. But where in a statute book would we look for the crime of subverting the laws of nature? What penalty would a court impose for killing off a geological epoch?

If not unlawful, then these acts are surely unethical. Yet to see them, as the dominant ethical theories would have it, as the result of a miscalculation about how to maximize human happiness or a failure to act according to a Kantian golden rule somehow trivializes the magnitude of what has been done. An ethical framework that can tell us whether it is wrong to overstate our travel expenses cannot tell us whether it is wrong to change the Earth's geological history. The attempt to frame it by mere ethics risks normalizing an event without parallel, of rendering prosaic a transition that is in fact Earth-shattering.

Before we apply existing ethical constructs to the Anthropocene, including the implied moral stance of those who dream of fleeing a dying Earth, we must grapple with the more foundational question thrown up by the new epoch: What kind of creature interfered with the Earth's functioning and would not desist when the facts become known? What kind of being made the laws and ethical codes and can now make plans to blast off into space or deploy its technological might to subdue the Earth through solar geoengineering? Who are we and what is the nature of our responsibility?

We begin to approach an answer when we understand human freedom as woven into the fabric of nature-as-a-whole, and how that truth was forgotten when we became besotted with our demands for freedoms and power over nature. It is only through a deep, pre-ethical sense of responsibility, lodged in the agent who accepts our collective embeddedness, that humans and nature can live together. This sense cannot belong to the individual or to the citizen of a nation (who is always inclined to shift responsibility to other nations), but to the human who feels the inescapable responsibility that comes with the unique and extraordinary place of humankind on planet Earth. And so, after the death of God, respect for the integrity of the Earth can grow only from the sense of gratitude for the gift of freedom and an acute awareness of its dangers. Such an orientation arises not from obligations to other humans (as in all conventional ethics), which is to say, not from the realm of freedom as such; it arises out of an understanding of freedom emerging from nature-as-a-whole.

For philosophers, evil is always a relation between humans inhabiting an inter-subjective world of their own making and so belongs to the domain of what humans do to each other. From this standpoint, it is because we are not natural that good and evil are possible in the world. Nothing an animal, let alone a force of nature, can do may be described as evil, a truth now commonplace enough but one belonging to a post-Renaissance world. Within an inter-subjective sphere it makes sense. Where humans act on the natural environment, on the other hand, our actions must be judged not according to where they fall on a scale of good and evil but where they fall on a scale of *care and neglect*. When humans formed an independent relation with the Earth, we were left to *choose* between a path of care and a path of neglect.

It was Kant's supreme insight that, for the enlightened human, freedom should be exercised within the constraints of self-imposed moral law. The moral law he had in mind, however, governed only our dealings with each other. If in the modern era freedom was understood as a relation between humans, as we enter the Anthropocene freedom must also, and primarily, be understood as it bears on our relationship with the Earth. The threat we present to the conditions of life is an expression of our agency, and any salvation can only be rooted in a radical change in how we understand and express our agency.

Freedom is always the freedom to destroy as well as create, and to destroy while creating. The worlds humans build may be in greater or lesser harmony with the constraints of nature's processes. So if we are free to care for nature we are also free to neglect it, to despoil, abuse, and ravage it. Neglect belongs to humankind alone because we are given our autonomy. Nothing else can take the blame for the despoliation of the planet, so there must be something in our destiny, woven as a possibility into nature, and now as an actuality, that frees us to decide to create or destroy.

As we enter the Anthropocene, mere neglect seems inadequate when confronted with the far-reaching and manifold damage humans have done to the natural world in full knowledge of the effects – not only by disrupting the climate but also by extinguishing species and spoiling large swathes of oceans, land, and air. In contrast to "casual neglect" arising from carelessness, the willful failure to respond to the mountain of evidence of Earth System destabilization might be dubbed *wanton neglect*, that is, both reckless and self-indulgent. Neglect becomes wanton not simply on the basis of its scale but when its consequences are known, and where that knowledge is derived from the gift of scientific understanding, which enables us to see, with amazing if far-from-perfect clarity, how the physical world works. Wanton neglect is the abuse of this gift, because we subordinate it to our desires.

This freedom-as-abandon is the defining feature of late modernity. Just as evil proclaims itself as one way of being free in the social world (the literary exemplar is the figure of Raskolnikov), so the wanton neglect of the natural world is a sublime expression of our freedom (whose exemplars can be found in real life but not yet in literature). To achieve this form of freedom one must decide to revel in one's autonomy without owning it, without taking responsibility for it. The predilection for care or neglect goes beyond morality; it expresses an orientation toward the natural world, to be in sympathy with it or to negate it. So I am not so much calling for a different kind of ethics; I am calling for a different kind of orientation to the Earth, one in which we understand deeply our extraordinary power and unique responsibility.

Wanton neglect should not be regarded as a deviation from the true nature of humans; it is in fact an *affirmation* of our true being – not in the sense that we are cursed by the urge to despoil but because the choices permitted by our agency reveal the essence of the human project, one that reaches its apogee in the conditions of late modernity. The openness given to humans to make the choice of how to care for the creation was the most tremendous ontological event. If we have taken the path of neglect, then that only affirms that freedom to care or neglect is inseparable from the being of humans. For humankind, how to create worlds while remaining within nature's limits and according to its rhythms is the supreme challenge.

Once humans had attained their majority – embracing a scientific understanding of the world and developing the technological power to transform nature – it was not inevitable that the species would develop and deploy its colossal power so recklessly as to cause the Earth to enter into a perilous new geological epoch. The gradual increase in greenhouse gas emissions, from the invention of James Watt's steam engine through to the Great Acceleration that followed World War II and which gathers pace even today in full knowledge of its hazards, was not the only path humans could have taken with their newfound freedom. While techno-industrialism and the structures of capitalism have powerful internal momentum, at every stage of development there have always been those calling for restraint. From the laments of the Romantic poets to the *Naturphilosophie* of the early nineteenth century, from

Walden to deep ecology, from the Club of Rome to contemporary climate activism, a chorus of protest could always be heard. At times the chorus has been loud enough to compel governments to join in. In 1987, the nations of the world endorsed the recommendations of the Brundtland Report on sustainable development. In 1992, the Framework Convention on Climate Change committed the world, in principle at least, to adopt measures to prevent dangerous climate change. And, in 2015, world leaders gathered in Paris to reaffirm their nations' pledges to work toward limiting global warming. So the campaigners have won some battles even if the war is not going well. Their efforts have been resisted at every stage by the forces of unrestrained expansion, so that every proposal to cut carbon emissions, for example, must be tempered by assurances that economic growth will not be impeded – which makes one wonder whether the world would merit saving if growth had to be slowed to save it.

There is a view that the carbon-intensive path to industrialization was unavoidable because it was only fossil energy that could power early factories. It is a strong argument, yet in the twentieth century a series of commercial and political decisions were made that could have seen the world swerve away from fossil energy. (France did.) Even now, cognisant of the dire consequences, decisions are still being made to privilege carbon-intensive energy sources. Vast new coalfields are being developed, along with new sources of carbon pollution like Canada's tar sands. For 20 years, George Mitchell doggedly pursued the engineering technology for hydraulic fracturing, convinced that the world would burn whatever new sources of petroleum and natural gas could be opened up. If not for luck and persistence his gamble could easily have been lost; but in the end it was vindicated, with a fracking boom in new forms of fossil-fuel extraction under way in North America, Europe, Australia, and beyond, promising to extend the fossil-fuel age by decades. It may be true that one cannot stop progress, but the form of progress has always been contestable and open to variations.

If responsibility requires both the freedom to act and the power to act, it also requires the inclination to act according to principle. One can immediately see the dilemma. Before Europeans came of age they looked to God, or at least the divine texts and their interpreters, for moral guidance. If the "death of God" was enough to give Europeans the freedom to act, and science and industry gave them the power, where could they find the principles and *motivation* to act responsibly?

Kant devoted himself to explaining how, after we had attained our majority, reason itself could impose on us a set of duties. Yet the search for morality in the principle of non-contradiction was always doomed. If his theory could provide a *reason*, it could not provide a *motive* to act in the social interest, let alone the interests of the Earth. The utilitarian's celebration of self-interest left responsibility to look after itself. As the intellectual justification for today's global markets it has proven catastrophic. For the economists whose minds have been shaped by utilitarianism, the millennial-scale destabilization of the Earth System due to carbon emissions is turned into an "externality," an effect that regrettably falls outside of the reach of markets and must therefore be brought into the utility-maximizing calculus of producers and consumers. In the deathless words of the Stern Review, climate change is "the greatest market failure the world has seen." Where warm-blooded human beings fit into this calculus is unclear.

Writing in the 1940s, Dietrich Bonhoeffer cautioned against "the shallow and banal this-worldliness of the enlightened, the busy, the comfortable, or the lascivious," and embodied a kind of Christian moral seriousness in which one does not shy from one's duties. But his Christian ethics, those of the Sermon on the Mount, were not strong enough to survive secularization. Similarly, Pope Francis's appeal to the love of nature, welcome as it is, is anchored in an era long-gone and rests on an authority most do not recognize.

For several decades, social democracy's pursuit of equality and the dignity of man survived by drawing on the moral legacy of Christianity, but by the 1970s it was too exhausted to resist being overwhelmed by neoliberal individualism. Social democratic thinkers now flail around looking for ways of coming to grips with the crisis of the Earth and end up in a social-only cul-de-sac.[13] Pale green environmentalism has attempted to fill the void, but its two motivations – enlightened self-interest and a love of nature – could have only limited appeal or limited success, while the ecocentrism of deep green philosophy seems to most to suppress the central fact of human uniqueness, and of subjectivity itself.

So I think we have to confront the most difficult truth – in the Anthropocene we have no ethical resources to draw on. The cupboard is bare. For all of their worthiness, appeals to "responsibility" have no heft, no ontological substance. Where once we could fear and love God and truly *believe* in him and his saving power, now we can only fear Gaia. But Gaia is no messiah, which leaves self-preservation as the only motive, a negative motive that seems much too weak. Unless, that is, we can become beings guided by a new cosmological sense rooted in the profound significance of humankind in the arc of the Earth.

So what do we do? A new ethics cannot be conjured out of words on a page, but awaits the realization that this being called human has become something strange and unfamiliar, a being who stands at the point of transition between two geological epochs – one provided by nature to allow it to flourish and the other, molded by it, that threatens to undo civilization. The question that now haunts the universe is whether, in allowing humans free will, "nature" made a colossal mistake. The arrival of the Anthropocene signals a moment in planetary history in which modernity's test is raised to an extreme degree. Are we to decide to press on doggedly with more of the same – more technological mastery, more exploitation of nature, more nihilism? Needless to say, this is the path of denial or willful recklessness for those who can only imagine a future as an enlarged version of the present, manufactured out of human ingenuity and resolve, even if it's a vision now known to be impossible to realize. Or will new human beings emerge who embody another future, who allow themselves to be appropriated by the next future, who are willing to think eschatologically – that is, to think the end of the world of techno-industrial appropriation in an era of trial and struggle, to accept that the Enlightenment did not banish all darkness and that the lamp of Reason shines too dimly to guide us through the night falling over us?

Living without Utopia ✓

How to finish a book like this? I don't know; it's too hard, too uncertain, too new. So let me just put down some last, stray thoughts, in the hope that they might stimulate better ones in the reader.

The arrival of the Anthropocene contradicts all narratives, philosophies, and theologies that foretell a preordained and continuous rise of humankind to ever-higher levels of material, social, or spiritual development. Stories of the irresistible triumph of humanity have themselves proven irresistible, from Hegel, Marx, Teilhard, and Maslow to metaphysical schemas of the "stages of consciousness" culminating in the divine or "superintegral." And, of course, their DNA can be found in their bastard child, modern growthism.

Those who live after the time of darkness and see only the time of light ahead are deaf to the "cry of the Earth" in Pope Francis's image; and isn't that true of every Modern? The passing of "the dark ages" and the arrival of the light of science, reason, modernity, and social progress took us beyond the anxiety of the "end times." We can no longer allow the possibility of regress, of the darkness returning; only the light can illuminate a path to the future.

There are those who believe salvation lies in the transcendent realm and those who want to make the transcendent immanent in this world. That modern political movements have a structure taken over from religion – the transcendent made immanent – may be a banal claim nowadays, but it serves to counter the more implausible belief that secularization took root because scientific facts proved that the transcendent realm was mere fantasy. The twentieth century was the century of ideologies promising Utopias on Earth. Each had found an essential flaw in the human world – the oppression of certain groups, insufficient economic development, a national historical grievance, a conspiracy of sinister forces – and each had the prescription for it. In all, however, the Earth was silently subsumed within the "order of being," which was confined to the two worlds, worldly and transcendent, whether the transcendent remained in the divine realm or had been immanentized into the mundane. But now, in the Anthropocene, that order of being – both its religious version as man's path to Heaven and its secular version as man's striving for worldly Utopias – is disturbed because a third active element has intruded, the Earth itself.

If utopian aspirations belong to the Holocene, what does it mean if we no longer believe in the light? It does not mean we must live in the darkness but that we must live in the half-light of not-knowing, in the new atmosphere of endangerment. It means we must learn to live on *this* world, as it really is, the immanent as immanent rather than the transcendent immanentized, as Bruno Latour has put it. Of course, this is the hardest task of all, for we have sandbagged our existence against the floodwaters of doubt with the forces of technology, production, progress, and self-determination. To learn to live in the doubt on a capricious Earth may take generations.

"Who will wipe the blood off us?" cried Nietzsche's madman. But perhaps there was no crime; the gods were not killed but simply withdrew, leaving for us the opportunity to create the future. By retreating they opened up something new on Earth, the prospect that humans could build new worlds emblazoned with hope. The opportunity has been seized beyond all imaginings; but only at the cost of jeopardizing the conditions of life on the planet. As we gaze into this Anthropocene century, we do not know our fate; it lies over the horizon. Perhaps there are new gods waiting there, strange gods whose plans for us we can only guess at.

This is the dispensation now returning, after progress: the rediscovery of the contingency of our existence in the cosmos, a contingency arising in the first place from the Earth System, an entity whose behavior reflects a precarious balance of enormously powerful forces and evades precise description, so that even the scientists most intimately familiar with its workings cast around for metaphors to capture its moods.

After the falling away of utopian dreams how do we respond to the return of this kind of contingency and endangerment? There is no precedent we can turn to. Most of us are unable to invest our faith in divine providence. The gods absconded long ago. Nor can the rupture in the comforting linearity of modern progress be answered by a return to a cyclical view of history, an eternal return of the same. Geology has taken care of that. Modernity, the era of self-assertion, in which the world took a break from teleology and opened up endless possibilities, is not returning to any kind of past known by humans. It remains a world of many possibilities except that now, to a disconcerting degree, some of the biggest "decisions" have been taken out of human hands and given back to the caprice of nature.

Can we find hope in this situation? If disturbance to the functioning of the Earth System is now to a greater or lesser degree irreversible, does this mean we must abandon ourselves to our fate? To do so would be to add moral cowardice to the list of infractions we already have to answer for. One thing is certain, though: the possibility of humanity's redemption does not provide for any kind of personal salvation. The hope of personal salvation is one more manifestation of the essence of modernity and its founding thought, the preoccupation with the self. The solipsism of modern consciousness followed on from our alienation from both the transcendent and nature so that freedom could be understood as a project of personal liberation. In the face of an impending disaster, saving oneself while others suffer has always been an unforgivable choice. Today we hear it in a new context, one no less indecent, when certain evangelical pastors declare: "I don't care about climate change. I will be in Heaven." To which one cannot help thinking that for one so callous the other place is the more deserved destination.

Whatever its personal consolations, rediscovering the gods will not stop the unfolding of the Anthropocene and its disruptions. The only response to the threats of the Anthropocene is a collective one, *politics*. It is true that history frequently frustrates the ambitions of those who want to hurry it along; but it can also surprise us by suddenly opening up. Ecological campaigners have not been able to prevent climate disruption, and turn the world from neglect to care, although advances have been made. Even so, they have prepared the soil for a turn in history, although no one knows when that turn will come, when there might be, in Hannah Arendt's well-chosen words, "an explosion of undercurrents which, having gathered their force in the dark, suddenly erupt."[14]

Barring the final cataclysm of an asteroid strike, the "end time" for humanity is likely to be a drawn-out era of struggle whose outcome is unknown. If there is to be retribution for the misuse of our freedom, then instead of a single day of judgment it will take the form of "a summary court in perpetual session," in Kafka's image. Perhaps humans always had to pass through the trials of the Anthropocene in order to arrive at a reconciliation between our almost limitless potentiality and appetites and the finitude of the Earth, a long and jagged "Fall" as an unavoidable stage in the moral progress of the species. The imposition of planetary boundaries by the Earth System in the Anthropocene, harsh as it will be, might be seen by its survivors as the path to true liberation, the cost of learning to live in solidarity with the Earth.

Can humankind be redeemed? Will humans be given another chance after the manifest failure to protect the Earth, to fulfill its purpose of evolving in concord with the Earth's benign possibilities? For those like Pope Francis who think in religious terms, "humanity has disappointed God's expectations," and they must wonder in their hearts whether the gods will finally turn away from their willful children and abandon them to their fate. The gods stand watching, in two minds. What would it mean for the cosmos to forsake humankind, they ask themselves, to allow it to ruin the Earth and deprive the cosmos of the being uniquely able to marvel at it and endow it with meaning? There is punishment enough to deal out; after all, the last million humans would suffice to fulfill the "telos" of the cosmos.

At times it seems impossible that this beautiful, shining planet should flower with a form of life endowed with the ability to render the universe knowable, only to see it withdraw into the darkness of unconsciousness. The hope this thought kindles is perhaps not one for our own futures, or for those of any descendants we can envision, but for another humanity, contrite and wiser. Having rejected their destiny as keepers of the planet, humans would then have been won over to it. There would, of course, be an eon of regret, of species-shame, in which humans experience the consequences of their neglect, before a process of repair and rejuvenation could occur. We cannot say that such a second civilization would vindicate the sorrows endured in the Anthropocene. The second civilization is too far off and uncertain for it to have any bearing on our times. We cannot picture that future realm of being; nor can we be sure that a resurrected humanity would take its second chance. If there is no guarantee of this eventuality, it nevertheless seems certain that those new humans, whose task is to build a new civilization from the planetary ashes of the old one, would look at those ashes and declare "Never again."

Notes

Preface: On Waking Up

1   Will Steffen, Jacques Grinevald, Paul Crutzen, and John McNeil, The Anthropocene: Conceptual and Historical Perspectives, *Philosophical Transactions of the Royal Society* A 369 (2011): 842–67, 843.
2   David Archer, *The Long Thaw* (Princeton, NJ: Princeton University Press, 2009), 149–57; Curt Stager, *Deep Future: The Next 10,000 Years of Life on Earth* (New York: Thomas Dunne Books, 2011), 34–42.
3   Hans-Georg Gadamer, *Truth and Method* (London: Bloomsbury, 1975), 61.
4   Martin Heidegger, *Contributions to Philosophy (Of the Event)* (Bloomington, IN: Indiana University Press, 2012), 279.

Chapter 1 The Anthropocene Rupture

1   Jan Zalasiewicz, Paul Crutzen, and Will Steffen, The Anthropocene. In F. M. Gradstein, J. G. Ogg, M. D. Schmitz, et al. (eds), *The Geologic Time Scale* (Boston, MA: Elsevier, 2012), 1033–40.
2   Will Steffen, Commentary on "The 'Anthropocene'." In Libby Robin, Sverker Sörlin, and Paul Warde (eds), *The Future of Nature:*

Documents of Global Change (New Haven, CT: Yale University Press, 2013), 487.

3 Statement by the International Geosphere-Biosphere Programme; available at: <http://www.igbp.net/globalchange/greatacceleration. 4.1b8ae20512db692f2a680001630.html>.

4 Jan Zalasiewicz et al., When Did the Anthropocene Begin? A Mid-Twentieth Century Boundary Level is Stratigraphically Optimal, *Quaternary International* 383 (October 5, 2015): 196–203.

5 James Syvitski, Anthropocene: An Epoch of Our Making, *Global Change* 78 (March 2012): 14.

6 Toby Tyrrell, Anthropogenic Modification of the Oceans, *Philosophical Transactions of the Royal Society* A 369 (2011): 887–908.

7 Peter U. Clark et al., Consequences of Twenty-First-Century Policy for Multi-Millennial Climate and Sea-Level Change, *Nature Climate Change* 6 (April 2016): 360–9, 360–1.

8 Charles H. Langmuir and Wally Broecker, *How to Build a Habitable Planet* (revised edition, Princeton, NJ: Princeton University Press, 2012), 645.

9 Jan Zalasiewicz, Mark Williams, Will Steffen, and Paul Crutzen, The New World of the Anthropocene, *Environmental Science and Technology* 44/7 (2010): 2228–31, 2231. Italics added.

10 Langmuir and Broecker, *How to Build a Habitable Planet*, 645.

11 Dipesh Chakrabarty, The Climate of History: Four Theses, *Critical Inquiry* 35/2 (2009): 197–222; Jacob Burckhardt, *Reflections on History* (Indianapolis, IN: Liberty Classics, 1979 [1868]), 31.

12 Kevin Trenberth, Framing the Way to Relate Climate Extremes to Climate Change, *Climatic Change*, November 115/2 (2012): 283–90.

13 Ian Angus, *Facing the Anthropocene: Fossil Capitalism and the Crisis of the Earth System* (New York: Monthly Review Press, 2016).

14 Paul Crutzen and Eugene Stoermer, The "Anthropocene", *Global Change Newsletter* 41 (2000): 17–18.

15 Clive Hamilton and Jacques Grinevald, Was the Anthropocene Anticipated? *The Anthropocene Review* 2/1 (April 2015): 59–72.

16 Quoted by Paul Edwards, *A Vast Machine: Computer Models, Climate Data, and the Politics of Global Warming* (Cambridge, MA: MIT Press, 2010), 67–9.

17 Spencer Weart, *The Discovery of Global Warming*, published online, 2012; available at: <https://www.aip.org/history/climate/climogy.htm>. (See also Spencer Weart, The Idea of Anthropogenic Global Climate Change in the 20th Century, *WIREs Climate Change* 1 (Jan/Feb 2010): 67–81.

18 With thanks to Jacques Grinevald for helping me refine these definitions.

19 Clive Hamilton, The Anthropocene as Rupture, *The Anthropocene Review* 2/1 (2016): 1–14.

20 William Ruddiman, The Anthropogenic Greenhouse Era Began Thousands of Years Ago, *Climatic Change* 61 (2003): 261–93.

21 Philippe Ciais, Christopher Sabine, Govindasamy Bala, Laurent Bopp et al., Carbon and Other Biogeochemical Cycles. In T. F. Stocker, D. Qin, G.-K. Plattner, M. Tignor, et al. (eds), *Climate Change 2013: The Physical Science Basis* (Cambridge: Cambridge University Press, 2013), 483–5 and Fig. 6.6.

22 Erle Ellis, Using the Planet, *Global Change* 81 (October 2013): 32–5.

23 T. M. Lenton and H. T. Williams, On the Origin of Planetary-Scale Tipping Points, *Trends in Ecology and Evolution* 28/7 (2013): 382. Note that for James Lovelock changes in the biosphere – which he uses in the narrow sense of the biota – can change the planet *because* they interact with the atmosphere and change the climate system.

24 Erle Ellis, Ecology in an Anthropogenic Biosphere, *Ecological Monographs* 85/3 (2015): 287–33, 288.

25 B. Smith and M. Zeder, The Onset of the Anthropocene, *Anthropocene* 4 (December 2013): 8–13, 8.

26   T. Braje and J. Erlandson, Human Acceleration of Animal and Plant Extinction: A Late Pleistocene, Holocene, and Anthropocene Continuum, *Anthropocene* 4 (December 2013): 14–23.

27   Simon Lewis and Mark Maslin, Defining the Anthropocene, *Nature* 519 (12 March 2015): 171–80. Lewis and Maslin were reprising the argument in R. Dull, R. Nevle, W. Woods, D. Bird, S. Avnery, and W. Denevan, The Columbian Encounter and the Little Ice Age: Abrupt Land Use Change, Fire, and Greenhouse Forcing, *Annals of the Association of American Geographers* 100/4 (2010): 755–71. For responses, see: Jan Zalasiewicz, Colin Waters, Anthony Barnosky, Alejandro Cearreta, et al., Colonization of the Americas, "Little Ice Age" Climate, and Bomb-Produced Carbon: Their Role in Defining the Anthropocene, *The Anthropocene Review* 2 (2015): 117–27; and Clive Hamilton, Getting the Anthropocene So Wrong, *The Anthropocene Review* 2 (2015): 102–7.

28   G. Certini and R. Scalenghe, Anthropogenic Soils and the Golden Spikes for the Anthropocene, *The Holocene* 21/8 (2011): 1269–74.

29   S. Gale and P. Hoare, The Stratigraphic Status of the Anthropocene, *The Holocene* 22/12 (2012): 1491–4.

30   Christophe Bonneuil and Jean-Baptiste Fressoz, *The Shock of the Anthropocene* (London: Verso, London, 2016), xi.

31   Bonneuil and Fressoz, *The Shock of the Anthropocene,* 170, 198.

32   Angus, *Facing the Anthropocene*.

33   Jedediah Purdy, *After Nature: A Politics for the Anthropocene* (Cambridge, MA: Harvard University Press, 2015), 16.

34   David Keith, *A Case for Climate Engineering* (Cambridge, MA: MIT Press, 2013), 170–2.

35   John Bellamy Foster, Brett Clark, and Richard York, *The Ecological Rift: Capitalism's War on the Earth* (New York: Monthly Review Press, 2010), 19–20.

36   Erle Ellis, The Planet of No Return, *Breakthrough Journal* (online) 2 (fall 2011).

37 Erle Ellis, Neither Good Nor Bad, *New York Times*, May 23, 2011.

38 Clive Hamilton, *Earthmasters: The Dawn of the Age of Climate Engineering* (London: Yale University Press, 2013), 90–2.

39 Peter Kareiva, Robert Lalasz, and Michelle Marvier, Conservation in the Anthropocene, *Breakthrough Journal* (online) 2 (fall 2011).

40 Erle Ellis, The Planet of No Return (my emphasis).

41 Bonneuil and Fressoz, *The Shock of the Anthropocene*, 289.

42 Andreas Malm and Alf Hornborg, The Geology of Mankind? A Critique of the Anthropocene Narrative, *The Anthropocene Review* 1/1 (2014): 62–9, 63.

43 Jason Moore, The Capitalocene, Part I: On the Nature & Origins of Our Ecological Crisis; available at: <http://www.jasonwmoore.com / uploads / The _ Capitalocene __ Part _ I __ June _ 2014 . pdf >, unpublished, undated, 4.

44 Paul Crutzen, Geology of Mankind, *Nature* 415 (2002): 23.

45 Bonneuil and Fressoz, *The Shock of the Anthropocene*, 66.

46 Jason Moore, The Capitalocene, Part I: On the Nature & Origins of Our Ecological Crisis; available at: <http://www.jasonwmoore.com / uploads / The _ Capitalocene __ Part _ I __ June _ 2014 . pdf >, unpublished, undated, 4.

47 Clive Hamilton, *Capitalist Industrialization in Korea* (Boulder, CO: Westview Press, 1986).

48 Alf Hornborg, Artifacts Have Consequences, Not Agency: Toward a Critical Theory of Global Environmental History, *European Journal of Social Theory* 20/1 (2017).

Chapter 2 A New Anthropocentrism

1 Vaclav Smil, Harvesting the Biosphere: The Human Impact, *Population and Development Review* 37/4 (December 2011): 613–36. The proportions are of mass measured in dry weight.

2 I'm grateful to Will Steffen for these points. He adds that the biosphere as a whole will adjust and will take part in the transition processes, but the survival of no element of it is guaranteed.

3 Jedediah Purdy, *After Nature: A Politics for the Anthropocene* (Cambridge, MA: Harvard University Press, 2015), dust jacket.

4 Pope Francis, *Laudato Si: On Care for Our Common Home* (published by the Vatican, May 24, 2015), 3, then 5 and 11.

5 With thanks to Bruno Latour for suggesting this image, without holding him responsible for the use I have made of it.

6 "But for Kant, the realm of morality is the realm of freedom, and freedom constitutes the human difference from the rest of nature." Michael Hogue, *The Tangled Bank: Towards an Ecotheological Ethics of Responsible Participation* (Eugene: Pickwick Publications, 2008), 191.

7 As Robin Attfield does in Beyond Anthropocentrism, *Royal Institute of Philosophy Supplement* 69 (October 2011): 29–46,.

8 John Passmore identified these in *Man's Responsibility for Nature: Ecological Problems and Western Traditions* (London: Duckworth, 1980, Appendix), along with two other kinds of anthropocentrism. In the first (due to Descartes), Nature was not made for man's use (and is in this sense not man-centered) but man should ruthlessly exercise his unique powers to transform and exploit nature. In the second (due to Berkeley-Kant), Nature does not exist "except insofar as man comes to bestow actuality on it."

9 Dipesh Chakrabarty, The Climate of History: Four Theses.

10 Malm and Hornborg, The Geology of Mankind? A Critique of the Anthropocene Narrative.

11 Lisa Sideris, Anthropocene Convergences: A Report from the Field. In Robert Emmett and Thomas Lekan (eds), *Whose Anthropocene? Revisiting Dipesh Chakrabarty's Four Theses*, RCC Perspectives: Transformations in Environment and Society, No. 2. (2016): 89–96.

12 Clive Hamilton, Theories of Climate Change, *Australian Journal of Political Science* 47/4 (2012): 721–9.

13 Clive Hamilton, *Requiem for a Species: Why We Resist the Truth about Climate Change* (London: Earthscan, 2010), ch. 4.

14 John Passmore writes (in *Man's Responsibility for Nature*, 179–80) that Hegel and Marx could see that it was in their ability to become civilized that humans added something to the world. "It is not merely out of arrogance that men think of themselves as having a 'duty to subdue nature'; it is only they who can create. So far, and only so far, they can rightfully claim 'Dominion over nature'."

15 Philippe Descola, *Beyond Nature and Culture* (Chicago, IL: University of Chicago Press, 2013), 121.

16 Erle Ellis, The Planet of No Return.

17 Michael Shellenberger and Ted Nordhaus, Love Your Monsters, Breakthrough Institute: available at: <http://thebreakthrough.org/index.php/journal/past-issues/issue-2/love-your-monsters>, November 29, 2011.

18 Although Tilley argues that the discourse on God and evil was not a perennial problem but only emerged during the Enlightenment. See Terrence Tilley, *The Evils of Theodicy* (Washington, DC: Georgetown University Press, 1991), 86, 229.

19 See Susan Neiman, *Evil in Modern Thought: An Alternative History of Philosophy* (Princeton, NJ: Princeton University Press, 2002), 86.

20 Ellis, The Planet of No Return.

21 G. W. F. Hegel, *Lectures on the Philosophy of World History: Introduction*, trans. H. B. Nisbet (Cambridge: Cambridge University Press, 1975), 43.

22 Neiman, *Evil in Modern Thought*, 69–70.

23 Paul Ricoeur, *The Symbolism of Evil* (New York: Harper & Row, 1967), 51.

24 Neiman, *Evil in Modern Thought*, 182.

25 Terry Eagleton, *Hope Without Optimism* (New Haven, CT: Yale University Press, 2015), 4.

26 Fredrik Albritton Jonsson, The Origins of Cornucopianism: A Preliminary Genealogy, *Critical Historical Studies* 1/1 (spring 2014): 151–68.

27 Clive Hamilton, *Earthmasters: The Dawn of the Age of Climate Engineering* (London: Yale University Press, 2013).

28 On Ruskin, see Vicky Albritton and Fredrik Albritton Jonsson, *Green Victorians: The Simple Life in John Ruskin's Lake District* (Chicago, IL: University of Chicago Press, 2016).

29 Adrian Wilding, Ideas for a Critical Theory of Nature, *Capitalism Nature Socialism* 19/4 (2008): 48–67.

Chapter 3 Friends and Adversaries

1 See: <http://news.xinhuanet.com/english/2009-12/27/content_127 11466.htm http://www.theguardian.com/environment/2009/dec/ 22/copenhagen-climate-change-mark-lynas>.

2 Hegel, *Lectures on the Philosophy of World History*, 197.

3 Clive Hamilton, *Growth Fetish* (London: Pluto Press, 2004).

4 To borrow Ollie Cussen's words from The Trouble with the Enlightenment, *Prospect Magazine* (May 5, 2013): available at: <http://www.prospectmagazine.co.uk/magazine/the-enlighten ment-and-why-it-still-matters-anthony-pagden-review>.

5 If the enforced spread of Western forms of democracy has often failed disastrously, the demand for justice can be heard everywhere.

6 Jason Moore, *Capitalism in the Web of Life* (London: Verso, 2015), 4.

7 Hornborg, Artifacts Have Consequences, Not Agency.

8 A point made by Ewa Domanska, Beyond Anthropocentrism in Historical Studies, *Historien* 10 (2010): 118–30, 118–19.

9 Domanska, Beyond Anthropocentrism in Historical Studies (my emphasis).

10 Michael Hardt and Antonio Negri, *Empire* (Cambridge, MA: Harvard University Press, 2000), 21.

11 Jane Bennett, *Vibrant Matter: A Political Ecology of Things* (Durham, NC: Duke University Press, 2009), 21.

12 Amanda Rees, Anthropomorphism, Anthropocentrism, and Anecdote: Primatologists on Primatology, *Science, Technology, & Human Values* 26/2 (spring 2001): 227–47, 228.

13 Donna Haraway, *The Companion Species Manifesto* (Chicago, IL: University of Chicago Press, 2003), 5.

14 Donna Haraway, Anthropocene, Capitalocene, Plantationocene, Chthulucene: Making Kin, *Environmental Humanities* 6 (2015): 159–65, 160.

15 "Dangerous extremists are using the very same argument of social construction to destroy hard-won evidence that could save our lives." Bruno Latour, Why Has Critique Run Out of Steam? From Matters of Fact to Matters of Concern, *Critical Inquiry* 30 (winter 2004): 225–8, 227.

16 Kieran Suckling, Against the Anthropocene, *Immanence*, blog post, July 7, 2014: available at: <http://blog.uvm.edu/aivakhiv/2014/07/07/against-the-anthropocene/> And a reply: Clive Hamilton, Anthropocene: Too Serious for Postmodern Games, *Immanence*, blog post, August 18, 2014: available at: <http://blog.uvm.edu/aivakhiv/2014/08/18/anthropocene-too-serious for-postmodern-games/>.

17 Anna Tsing, Unruly Edges: Mushrooms as Companion Species, *Environmental Humanities* 1 (2012): 141–54, 145.

18 Tim Morton, Anna Lowenhaupt Tsing's *The Mushroom at the End of the World: On the Possibility of Life in Capitalist Ruins*, *Somatosphere* (website), December 8, 2015. Available at: <http://somatosphere.net/2015/12/anna-lowenhaupt-tsings-the-mushroom-at-the-end-of-the-world-on-the-possibility-of-life-in-capitalist-ruins.html>.

19   Timothy James LeCain, Against the Anthropocene. A Neo-Materialist Perspective, *International Journal for History, Culture and Modernity* 3/1 (2015): 1–28.

20   Moore, The Capitalocene, Part I.

21   Jason Moore, *Capitalism in the Web of Life* (London: Verso, 2015), 171.

22   Moore, *Capitalism in the Web of Life*, 172–3.

23   Latour, Why Has Critique Run Out of Steam?, 232.

24   Anna Tsing, A Feminist Approach to the Anthropocene: Earth Stalked by Man (lecture at Barnard College, November 10, 2015); available at: <https://vimeo.com/149475243>.

25   Haraway, Anthropocene, Capitalocene, Plantationocene, Chthulucene, 159.

26   Hornborg, Artifacts Have Consequences, Not Agency.

27   Descola, *Beyond Nature and Culture*, 86.

28   Bruno Latour, How To Make Sure Gaia is Not a God of Totality? Unpublished lecture to a conference in Rio de Janeiro, September 2014.

29   Latour, How To Make Sure Gaia is Not a God of Totality?

30   Descola, *Beyond Nature and Culture*, 121.

31   Descola, *Beyond Nature and Culture*, 86; emphasis added.

32   Descola, *Beyond Nature and Culture*, 87.

33   Descola, *Beyond Nature and Culture*, 405.

34   Descola, *Beyond Nature and Culture*, 85.

35   Descola, *Beyond Nature and Culture*, 85.

36   Lucas Bessire and David Bond, 'Ontological Anthropology and the Deferral of Critique', *American Ethnologist* 41/3 (2014): 440–56, 445.

37   Bruno Latour, *An Inquiry into Modes of Existence: An Anthropology of the Moderns* (Cambridge, MA: Harvard University Press, 2015), 182.

Chapter 4 A Planetary History

1 Friedrich Nietzsche, *On Truth and Lies in an Extra-Moral Sense*. In *The Portable Nietzsche*, edited and translated by Walter Kaufmann (Harmondsworth: Penguin, 1977), 46–7.

2 Carl Sagah, *Cosmus* (New York: Random House, 1980), 7.

3 John Gray, *Straw Dogs* (London: Granta Books, 2002), 151. Terry Eagleton commented: "His book is so remorselessly, monotonously negative that even nihilism implies too much hope" (*Guardian*, September 7, 2002).

4 John Hick, *Evil and the God of Love* (London: Macmillan, 1985 [1966]), 256.

5 See John Hick's influential *Evil and the God of Love*, especially 253ff. Mark Scott argues that such a theodicy is better founded on the theology of Origen – Mark Scott, Suffering and Soul-Making: Rethinking John Hick's Theodicy, *The Journal of Religion* 90/3 (2010): 313–34. Terrence Tilley argues that Irenaeus was not doing theodicy at all and that Hick was reading theodicy into his writings – *The Evils of Theodicy*, 228.

6 Bruno Latour, *Facing Gaia* (Cambridge: Polity, 2017).

7 E. H. Carr, *What Is History?* (Harmondsworth: Penguin, 1964), 134.

8 Slavoj Žižek, *Less Than Nothing: Hegel and the Shadow of Dialectical Materialism* (London: Verso, 2013), 213.

9 Žižek, *Less Than Nothing*, 217.

10 T. S. Eliot quoted by Žižek, *Less Than Nothing*, 208.

11 Catherine Malabou, *The Future of Hegel: Plasticity, Temporality and Dialectic,* trans. Lisabeth During (London: Routledge, 2005), 13.

12 Karl Barth, *God Here and Now* (London: Routledge & Kegan Paul, 1964), 37.

13 Quoted by Martin Heidegger in *Schelling's Treatise on the Essence of*

Human Freedom, translated by Joan Stambaugh (Athens, OH: Ohio University Press, 1985 [1971]), 1. Heidegger himself commented on "the profound untruth of those words."

Chapter 5 The Rise and Fall of the Super-agent

1   Hans Jonas, Life, Death, and the Body in the Theory of Being, *The Review of Metaphysics* 19/1 (September 1965): 3–23, 3.

2   The expression is due to Bruce Matthews, *Schelling's Organic Form of Philosophy* (Albany, NY: State University of New York, 2011), 34. See F. W. J. Schelling, *Philosophical Investigations into the Essence of Human Freedom* (Albany, NY: State University of New York Press, 2006 [1809]), 73f. My reading of Schelling has been influenced by Heidegger's *Schelling's Treatise on the Essence of Human Freedom*.

3   Beginning with Schelling (see Matthews, *Schelling's Organic Form of Philosophy*, 4) and reaching a clarity with Schopenhauer (see Clive Hamilton, *The Freedom Paradox: Towards a Post-Secular Ethics* (Sydney: Allen & Unwin, 2008), 98–9).

4   The arguments elaborated in the next two paragraphs were suggested by Bruno Latour.

5   Arthur Schopenhauer, *The World as Will and Representation* (New York: Dover Publications, 1969), II, 196.

6   Quoted by Matthews, *Schelling's Organic Form of Philosophy*, 30.

7   Matthews, *Schelling's Organic Form of Philosophy*, 2.

8   Hamilton, *Earthmasters*, 90–2.

9   Kaya Burgess, Space Ark Will Save Man from a Dying Planet, *The Times*, April 28, 2014.

10 See: <http://projectpersephone.org/pmwiki/pmwiki.php>.

11 Paul Tillich, *The Future of Religions* (New York: Harper & Row, 1966), 43.

12 Burgess, Space Ark Will Save Man from a Dying Planet (emphasis added).

13 Ulrich Beck looked for the answer to climate change in "the power and conflict dynamics of social inequalities," ending up *welcoming* the climate crisis because it opens industrial modernity to a process of "self-dissolution and self-transformation." Anthony Giddens, bewitched by denialist claims that the science is disputed, wants to find a Third Way through the "scientific controversies," concluding that "there is another world waiting for us out there," one to be found via a "cross-party framework" (but one excluding Greens who are beyond the pale). See Hamilton, Theories of Climate Change.

14 Hannah Arendt, *The Human Condition* (Chicago, IL: University of Chicago Press, 2013), 248.

Index

INDEX

178

INDEX